i

you are hereby
invited to:

Come & See

Come & See!

You've been issued an invitation to come and see; now you have a choice to make. Will you come? Will you come with your eyes open, wanting to see? If you decide to come, it means leaving where you are for someplace new. This can be both exciting and intimidating, can't it? Will the place you are going be worth the effort? It doesn't feel safe, and definitely not comfortable. But to get someplace new, you've got to leave the old behind. I'll try to make starting easier by answering some questions you might have.

Where Are We Going?

We're headed into the Gospel of John. The word "Gospel" means good news. The good news John wants to share with us is that the only God, whom we cannot see, sent His Son as a human who could be seen, in order to make Himself known. God sent Jesus to show us who He is, so that we could see, believe, and through believing, have life in His name.

John's Gospel reads somewhat like a courtroom trial. The prologue comprises the opening arguments, the conclusion contains the closing arguments, and the middle is full of eyewitness testimony and evidence to support the case. If John's Gospel reads like a trial, what is it that's on trial? The identity of Jesus. He claimed to be the Messiah the Jews had been waiting for. He claimed to be God. Both claims are big and come with significant implications. John writes to prove that Jesus is who He claimed to be.

Often, as John lays out the evidence to make his case, he does something interesting. John switches up the trial and put his readers on the stand. Having seen the evidence, what will their response be?

Follow the trial. Weigh the evidence. Arrive at your verdict. **Come & See!**

How Will We Get There?

For the brief time Jesus walked this earth, God could be seen in human flesh. Now we see God through His Word; it's how He's chosen to reveal Himself to us. So the path to relationship with God is walked out on the pages of the Bible. That's why some form of Bible study is important.

Following a structured study can be intimidating because it suggests accountability. Do you have visions of someone looking over your shoulder, keeping score? That won't happen, I promise.

We're all busy with more to do than we have time for, so, just as in other areas of life, in Bible study we need to strike an appropriate balance. You'll never *find* time for anything important. You have to *make* time. Making time involves making choices. We get a set amount of time each day so we have to choose what we'll make time for and what we won't. This is where things can get tricky. Jobs, kids, school, eating, sleeping—these are non-negotiables. But we all have things competing for our time and attention that are negotiable.

With this balancing act in mind, there are several levels of study you can commit to:

1. Watch the teaching sessions available at www.unshakenministries.com. Each session contains a summary of the week's learning, so even if this is all you are able to do, you'll end up with an overarching picture of John's Gospel. You'll notice the teaching session guides are an outline of the main topics covered, followed by a page for taking notes. If you're a note-taker, we've given you room, so scribble away. If you'd rather sit back and listen, the main ideas are there for you to refer back to as needed.
2. Watch the teaching sessions and memorize the verse of the week—these are the verses found in a box at the bottom of the introductory page for each week of homework.
3. Watch the teaching sessions and read the Gospel of John at the pace of the study.
4. Watch the teaching sessions and complete the weekly homework. Direction, not perfection, is the goal. If some weeks you only complete a day of homework, and other weeks you don't write down a single word but only read through the homework, that's okay, you're still learning and growing.
5. *New and exciting:* go to www.unshakenministries.com and watch/listen to discussion surrounding the homework material. We'll be posting short videos that correlate with the homework, meaning that you can interact with it even when you're busy and on the go. If sitting down with a book and a pen doesn't fit into your schedule, you can follow along during your daily commute or while making supper!
6. Any combination of the above.

Prayerfully give the specifics of your heart and your circumstances to God, asking Him to reveal the best path for you. Then choose your path—not from guilt, but from the freedom you have in Christ. Our Saviour is gentle with us. But He is also doing His work in us, and growth requires stretching.

What Will the Road Be Like?

Have you noticed how, when people plan journeys that take them from where they are to someplace new, they often invite others to come with them? Either by physically inviting others along for the trip, or by including them through picture or video? We do this because we're built for relationship; we want community. So if you're able to come and see in community, that would be great. You could find or create a church group, a neighbourhood group, a work group, some friends, some family, or any combination you're able to imagine, and invite them to do the study together with you. You can also join in or create community by interacting with videos on the website or social media pages. Journeying together provides us with encouragement and accountability. Much of our spiritual growth is individual and happens between us and God in the quiet times, alone, while reading His Word or in prayer. But God made us for community, so we also grow stronger together.

If you're part of a group, it's recommended that you meet once a week to discuss what you're learning before watching the weekly teaching session. You likely won't have time to discuss everything covered in the homework, so your discussion time could be guided by discussing the reflection and application questions from day five, as well as by looking for *statements that look like this, which can be good jumping-off points for conversation.*

You're still reading so it seems likely you've taken up the invitation to come & see. I'm excited for what God will reveal of Himself to you. It's no small thing to encounter the God of glory – you'll never be the same!

Arlene Bergen

Now Jesus did many other signs in the presence of the disciples,

which are not written in this book;

but these are written so that you may believe that Jesus is the Christ,

the Son of God,

and that by believing you may have life in his name.

John 20:30-31

Table of Contents

Teaching Session One: In the Beginning (John 1:1-18)

❖ John intentionally opens his Gospel with the same three words that open Jewish Scriptures: "In the beginning." He purposely points his Jewish readers back to Genesis 1:1: *In the beginning God created the heavens and the earth.*

   ◆ He's pointing all readers to the truth that if everything is from God, it is also all for God.

*There is one God, the Father, **from whom** are all things and **for whom** we exist. 1 Corinthians 8:6*

   ◆ Your life is not random meaningless chance. It is the spectacular one-of-a-kind creative work of God.

❖ **WHAT:** The identity of Jesus is what's on trial.

❖ **WHO:** John's witness will hold significant weight in this trial, so who was he?
   ◆ John had a close, intimate friendship with Jesus and referred to himself as the disciple whom Jesus loved. (John 13:23; 19:26; 20:2; 21:20)
   ◆ John was an eyewitness to the trial and crucifixion of Jesus, and took Jesus' mother, Mary, to live with him in his own home. (John 18:15; 19:27, 35)
   ◆ John was an elder in the early church and devoted the rest of his life to spreading the good news about who Jesus was.

❖ **WHEN:** John wrote his gospel between 80-90 A.D.

❖ **WHERE:** The Gospel of John was likely written from the city of Ephesus—an important port city in the Roman Empire where John lived.

❖ **WHY:**

Now Jesus did many other signs in the presence of the disciples, which are not written in this book; but these are written so that you may believe that Jesus is the Christ, the Son of God, and that by believing you may have life in his name. John 20:30-31

❖ The Messiah is Jesus—He's the One all of history has been waiting for. This is the truth, and it's the best news because it's literally life or death.

❖ John, the other disciples, and early church leaders were fully convinced that Jesus is who He said, and they lived and died with the full assurance of their faith.
  ◆ Coming to believe Jesus' claims about who He is will take faith, but not blind faith.

❖ John uses the word "signs" in his purpose statement because signs are not *the* point or the destination, rather they point to or lead *towards* the destination.
  ◆ John wants his readers to see that the point of every miracle Jesus did wasn't the miracle itself. The miracles were always signs pointing to something and someone far greater.

And the Word became flesh and dwelt among us, and we have seen his glory, glory as of the only Son from the Father, full of grace and truth. John 1:14

❖ The Word took on flesh and lived with us.
  ◆ The incarnation simply refers to Jesus keeping all the fullness of being God while also taking on flesh and the limitations of humanity.
  ◆ Creation deals in physical realities; the incarnation deals in spiritual realities.

❖ What happens when God dwells with humanity? We can catch a glimpse of what it will be like in Revelation 21:3, when God will finally and forever dwell with man: He will wipe away every tear, He will do away with death, mourning, crying, and pain.
  ◆ These are the very things that characterized Jesus' ministry on earth.

For the law was given through Moses; grace and truth came through Jesus Christ. John 1:17

❖ For the first time we see who the Word is: Who was at the beginning, with God? Who was God? Who made all things? Who has life and light inside of Himself? Who is the light that overcame darkness? Who came into the world He created to invite all who believe in Him into His family? **Jesus Christ.**
  ◆ He was the One the Law had been pointing to all along, and He fulfilled the Law.

No one has ever seen God; the only God, who is at the Father's side, he has made him known. John 1:18

❖ Jesus came to make God known.

Session Notes:

_____

_____

_____

_____

_____

_____

_____

_____

_____

_____

_____

_____

_____

_____

_____

_____

_____

_____

_____

_____

_____

_____

_____

_____

WEEK ONE: FIRST THINGS

If John's Gospel reads like a courtroom trial and Chapter 1:1-18 consists of the opening arguments, then the verses immediately following signal that the trial has begun. John is ready to call his first witnesses to the stand and to present the first pieces of evidence.

John's purpose is clear; he is writing his Gospel to show readers that the Messiah they have been waiting for is Jesus. To establish this truth, John will rely on several key pieces of evidence: the testimony of eyewitnesses who encountered Jesus, the words of Jesus about Himself, the words of God about Jesus, the evidence of the Scriptures and their fulfillment in Jesus, and the works of Jesus—the miracles which John calls "signs." This week in our homework, we will see at least one piece of evidence from each category.

First impressions are important. Come & See!

In the beginning was the Word, and the Word was with God, and the Word was God.
He was in the beginning with God.
All things were made through him, and without him was not any thing made that was made.
John 1:1-3

Day One: First Witness—John the Baptist (John 1:19-28)

Don't you just love a good courtroom drama? My favourite books, movies, and television shows come from this genre of entertainment and seeing that this category often tops the ratings, I'm not alone in feeling this way. My guess is, we are drawn in by the lure of mystery—who did it, how did they do it, and why? If you're like me, you can get caught up in playing the parts of lawyer, judge, and jury, picking apart evidence and witnesses while trying to figure out who is innocent and who isn't. It's satisfying when the mystery is unraveled, truth is revealed, and justice prevails.

I suspect most of us will only experience the thrill of a courtroom from the comfort of our sofas. If you don't fall into that category and you're a real lawyer or judge, or someone else informed in legal proceedings from more than TV, books, and Google, I need to warn you: there may be material coming up that could lead to excessive eye-rolling because of my media-driven understanding of law and order. I've never been to law school or read a legal book that wasn't a novel or a true crime story. I owe you an apology if I've reduced your hard work to its Hollywood version.

But, from the comfort of my couch cushions, I feel like I've discovered some important truths. In a trial, testimony is important, especially eyewitness testimony. And the more critical the testimony, the more weight is placed on the character of the person standing behind it. Evidence is critical, and any evidence submitted needs to be able to support the case and be solid, irrefutable.

With all the courtroom drama available for our entertainment, we could probably talk about this for days. But what does this have to do with our study in the Gospel of John? In the introduction, we saw that John's Gospel is written somewhat like a courtroom trial. The identity of Jesus is put on the stand and witnesses are called to testify—is Jesus the Messiah He claimed to be? John wants to use his eyewitness testimony to show us that Jesus is the Son of God who came to love us, redeem us, and reveal God the Father to us. John wants his readers to see and hear Jesus, and to believe that He is who He said He was.

Now Jesus did many other signs in the presence of the disciples, which are not written in this book; but these are written so that you may believe that Jesus is the Christ, the Son of God, and that by believing you may have life in his name. John 20:30-31

Today we open our Bibles to John 1:19-28 and take our seat at the proceedings. Let's listen to the questions asked of the first eyewitness and hear his response. Then, we'll weigh the evidence.

1. Read John 1:19-28.
   a. This is the (what) _____ of (who) _____? (verse 19)

   b. Who's asking the question?

   c. What is the question?

Good lawyers know that to establish the truth of their position, they have to put the right witnesses on the stand. Once a witness is called, it's the lawyer's job to ask good questions to draw out what the witness knows and how it relates to the case.

The priests and Levites seem like they're asking a reasonable question, don't they? After all, they were the religious leaders of the day. Their job was to act like the temple police – to monitor religious activity and keep their finger on the pulse of the people. It was their job to know what kind of prophets were among the people, and what these prophets were saying – the claims they were making.

Yes, at this point in the trial, it seems the priests and the Levites are doing a commendable job of seeking the truth and making sense of the evidence with the question they ask.

2. Referencing John 1:19-28, answer the following questions.
   a. How does John the Baptist answer the question?

   b. Concluding that he is not the Christ, which two Old Testament figures do they think John might be?

   c. How does he answer both of these questions?

Do these questions seem stranger than the first? To our ears, it's a bit harder to determine whether or not these are good questions. After John the Baptist declares that he is not the Christ, the Messiah, why do the religious leaders follow up by asking if he's Elijah or the Prophet?

3. To weigh the merit of these questions, we need to find out some more about John the Baptist.
    a. John the Baptist's birth announcement is recorded in Luke 1:5-25. Feel free to read all of it, but what do you learn about him from verses 16 and 17, specifically?

    b. Read Matthew 11:7-15. Who does Jesus say John is in verse 14?

4. Let's look a little closer at why the Jewish religious leaders asked John the Baptist if he was Elijah.
    a. Compare 2 Kings 1:8 and Matthew 3:4. What do we learn about the appearance of both Elijah and John the Baptist?

    b. In Malachi 4:5-6, what does God say He will do and why?

5. Based on Deuteronomy 18:15 and 18, why do you think Jewish religious leaders would have wondered if John the Baptist was the Prophet?

With more background information, we can see that the religious leaders were still asking good questions. Jewish people of that time knew both their history and their Scriptures.

They knew Moses as the hero of faith God used to deliver His people from slavery in Egypt, and through whom God revealed His Law which set out how the Jewish people were to live.

They knew Elijah as the prophet who spoke words from God to His people during the time of Israel's wickedest king. God used Elijah to urge His people away from divided hearts and insincere worship, towards repentance. When Elijah's job was done, he bypassed death when God took him to heaven in a fiery chariot. (2 Kings 2:11)

Moses and Elijah were both important historical figures to the people of Israel. But there was more to it than that. Both of these men were associated with a coming — a return. Another prophet like Moses was coming. One like Elijah was coming back. At this point in history, the anticipation related to these historical figures was as big — maybe even bigger than the individuals themselves. Both men were associated with signs that pointed to the coming of the day of the LORD.

This was the Day the Jewish people waited for. Yes, they had returned to their Promised Land from exile, but still they waited because their land was ruled by Romans. Yes, their worship was once again centred around a temple, but still they waited because this temple had never seen a visible manifestation of God's glory.

They waited because their Scriptures told them a better time was coming. A time when the law would not be restricted to tablets of stone but would be fleshed out and written on their hearts (Jeremiah 31:34). A time when the LORD would comfort His people by bringing them salvation (Isaiah 52) through a suffering servant (Isaiah 53 and 54) who would extend an invitation to all people (Isaiah 55 and 56), culminating in a future glory that far exceeded their current reality (Isaiah 60-66).

The religious leaders were waiting and watching for signs of something greater, so they asked questions, attempting to make sense of their times. When they saw that a growing crowd was following John the Baptist, they knew it was their job to find out who he was.

John was clear who he was not. But telling someone who you are not, does not answer who you are.

6. According to John 1:22, why are they asking the question?

7. Fill in the blanks from John 1:22: What do _____ say about _____?

8. What is John's response?

John answers their question about who he is by referring to the words of a prophet. He draws their attention to a passage of Scripture that had been written by the prophet Isaiah centuries earlier. As God's mouthpiece, Isaiah warned the people repeatedly that if they did not turn from their wicked and rebellious ways they would be taken into exile—forcibly removed from their Promised Land. That's what the first 39 chapters of Isaiah speak about.

Then, at the beginning of Chapter 40, there is an abrupt change. Through the mouth of the same prophet, God tells His people that, yes, they will be taken into exile. But there will be a way of return—another exodus.

9. Turn to the passage John the Baptist was referring to in Isaiah 40:1-5.
    a. Whose way is being prepared? (verse 3)

    b. What will be revealed? (verse 5)

    c. Who will see it? (verse 5)

    d. Who has declared it? (verse 5)

10. Who is John the Baptist pointing to with his answer?

Eyewitnesses aren't put on the stand to talk about themselves. They are not the focus of the trial or the point of the questions. The only reason they are called to the stand is to point to the one they testify about. The religious leaders have come to John because they are looking for, and waiting for, the Messiah. John is clear with them that he is not the one they are waiting for. He is the one preparing the way for the Messiah. Do you know what that means? *He's coming*!

The One they have waited for is coming and is already among them.

John's voice crying out in the wilderness is a warning that they must be prepared because the time for another exodus has come—an exodus from the slavery of sin to the freedom of salvation.

The grass withers, the flower fades, but the word of our God will stand forever. Isaiah 40:8
And the Word became flesh and dwelt among us . . . John 1:14

The trial has begun. The first witness has been called. As you follow this trial, put yourself on the stand. Ask yourself important questions.

Who do you believe Jesus to be? Has His life impacted yours? What is your response?

The question of who Jesus Christ is holds the weight of eternity in the balance so it's imperative that we ask good questions and look for good answers. Once the evidence of Scripture is examined, we need to respond. We can disregard or disbelieve the evidence and choose to live for ourselves and for what the world offers. Or, we can see and believe that Jesus is who He says He is. But we can't do both.

The God of our fathers appointed you to know his will, to see the Righteous One and to hear a voice from his mouth; for you will be a witness for him to everyone of what you have seen and heard. And now why do you wait? Rise and be baptized and wash away your sins, calling on his name. Acts 22:14-16

Day Two: First Evidence—Look! The Lamb of God! (John 1:29-34)

Words, phrases, symbols—they all carry significance. That's why we use them. Sometimes their meaning is tied to cultures, periods of time, or specific geographical regions so that the weight of their meaning relies on context.

I am Canadian. My country is not known for its patriotism. We are mostly a humble, quiet people. Some of our national symbols include the maple leaf, maple syrup, our hockey teams, and the beaver. (If you're not Canadian and think this is a typo, I understand. It takes a special country to pick a large, industrious rodent as a national symbol.)

For the most part, Canadians don't draw much attention to, or get wrapped up in emotionalism surrounding the ties that bind us. (Except hockey. We're pretty loud about hockey.) But something that brings a tear to the most hardened Canadian eye, something that unites us from coast to coast, is the feeling of belonging we get when we step into a Tim Horton's. This fast-food restaurant (started by a hockey player!) serves mediocre coffee and donuts, but it stirs up our national pride. If you mention the possibility of a "Timmies run," and get a blank stare, you're not talking to a Canadian.

Canadians who've been abroad will, upon coming home, post the obligatory picture of themselves clutching a "Timmies" to announce they've returned. It's a bold statement: this is who I am. This is where I belong.

The people of Israel had quite a list of things that united them—things that distinguished them from the people around them, formed their national identity, and defined who they were. The book of Exodus is one place we can go to learn about some of the symbols and ceremonies that united the people of Israel. Because it gives us some of the story behind the story, it's a great place to turn for corroborating evidence.

Perhaps the greatest feature that defined and united them was their system of sacrifice. They weren't the only people group of the day with a system of sacrifice. Most ancient cultures had some series of rituals they performed to appease their gods. Israel's system, however, was distinct. They sacrificed to One God, not many. And they had no image or re-creation of the God they sacrificed to; it was forbidden. How do you make an image of a God who has made all that exists but was not Himself made; a God that can't be seen? The people of Israel did not guess at their sacrifices, hoping to appease a pantheon of unpredictable, unstable gods. Their God, the only true God, gave them His Law to reveal who He is—Holy. He gave them the system of sacrifice to show them who they were—rebellious. God's Law established the system of sacrifice to pave the way for sinful people to be in relationship with Holy God. At the centre of this entire system of sacrifice was the lamb. There were other animals sacrificed, yes, but the lamb was central.

Why? Because the event that most defined and shaped their national identity was their deliverance from slavery in Egypt. It was pivotal. In fact, the month they were delivered from Egypt by the hand of God became the first month of the year for them. (Exodus 12:2)

We find the account of the exodus in the second book of the Bible. The first book, Genesis, tells the story of the patriarchs, the men from whom the nation of Israel came. Genesis ends with the people of Israel moving to Egypt under the direction of the patriarch Joseph to escape famine in the land of Canaan. There they lived under the favour of the Pharaoh.

About four hundred years pass between Genesis and Exodus, so by the time Exodus opens, things have changed. The Pharaoh no longer remembers Joseph. The people of Israel have grown in number and Pharaoh fears they'll rise up against him. So, he enslaves them and mistreats them terribly. He even goes so far as to instruct Hebrew midwives to kill all baby boys after they're born. The people of Israel are in a bleak and hopeless situation. Until God steps in.

1. Turn to Exodus 3:7-8.
    a. What does God say He has seen?

    b. What has He heard?

    c. What does He know?

    d. What will He do?

2. God will use Moses and his brother Aaron to accomplish this deliverance. Turn to Exodus 4.
    a. What does God tell Moses to take with him in verse 17, and for what purpose is he to use it?

    b. According to verse 28, what does Moses tell Aaron when they meet up in the desert?

    c.   What does verse 30 tell us Moses and Aaron did upon returning to the Israelites?

    d.   What word shows up in all three of the verses above?

3.   In Exodus 5:1-2, what reason does Pharaoh give for not listening to Moses and Aaron?

4.   God responds in Exodus 6:5-7. What does He want His people to know?

A series of plagues follows. Pharaoh sometimes relents for a moment, just to make the plague go away. But as soon as he experiences physical relief, his spirit is hardened once again. The first three plagues fall on all people in both Egypt and Goshen. Things change with the fourth plague.

5.   Read Exodus 8:22-23.
    a.   God had told Moses to tell Pharaoh what would happen if he continued to refuse to let His people go. What does God say He will now do in verse 23?

    b.   Why will He do this, according to the end of verse 22?

In each of the remaining plagues, God distinguishes between His people and the people of Egypt. He does this to show both the Egyptians and His people who He is and what He is like.

Pharaoh still doesn't listen. God threatens to send a final plague of death that would fall on every household. Unless… There was only one way to escape the sureness of coming death.

6.   Read Exodus 12:1-13 and summarize the way in which they could escape the judgment of the angel of death as it passed through the land.

In a time of great distress and bondage, God saw, heard, and knew. He did not turn His back on His people. He came down to deliver them. God knew that His people needed to see signs that pointed to who He was before they would trust Him to deliver them. So He gave them signs. In the final, most devastating sign of all, God showed them that the only escape from death was by seeking refuge under the blood of a perfect lamb.

This night was the turning point in their national story. From that time on, the people of Israel began their year by remembering how judgment fell on a perfect lamb and spared them.

After the people of Israel escaped the bondage of Egypt, they were led into the wilderness to worship God and receive His Law which outlined the system of sacrifice.

7. Beside the following references, jot down the idea or meaning the people of Israel would have associated with the image of a lamb.

   a. Exodus 29:38-39

   b. Leviticus 14:12-13

   c. Isaiah 53 was a well-known passage among the Jewish people because it gave them a description of the coming Messiah. What association do you see between the Messiah and the lamb in Isaiah 53:7?

8. Now that we have a deeper understanding of the significance of the lamb, read John 1:29-34.

   a. The passage begins with the phrase, "The next day . . ." The next day after what?

   b. Fill in the blanks: "Look, the _____ of _____, who _____ _____ the _____ of the _____." (John 1:29)

John the Baptist points to Jesus and declares to people who are under the political bondage of Rome and under the eternal bondage of sin and death, *Look! Your Lamb has come. This man is God's Lamb who will take away the sins of the world.*

Jesus was the Lamb of the morning and evening sacrifice. Jesus was the Lamb offered as a guilt offering, as the sin offering. Jesus was the Lamb of Isaiah 53 who was oppressed and afflicted but did not open His mouth. Jesus was the Lamb whose blood covers all who come to Him for protection from the judgment of God.

The day before, John had been asked, "Who are you?" In his response, he focused more on who he was not. To answer who he was, John said he was a voice preparing the way. The very next day, John points to Jesus and says, "Look!" John then defines, as best as he is able, who Jesus is.

9. Read John 1:31-34.

    a. What was John the Baptist doing in this passage?

    b. Why was he doing it?

    c. What evidence did John have confirming Jesus as the Son of God?

I love the witness of John the Baptist in this passage.

This is who He is. This is how I know.
This now defines my purpose.
Therefore, I will testify.

John was single-minded in his purpose because he knew beyond a question of doubt **Who** defined him. His faith was not blind. It was backed by physical evidence. With his own ears he heard the voice speaking from heaven. His own eyes saw the dove descend and remain. This knowing for certain made him bold in his testimony and clear in his purpose. His job was to reveal the Messiah to Israel. Not to be Him. Not to explain Him. Not to imitate Him. John knew he was to be a sign pointing to the One all of history pointed to.

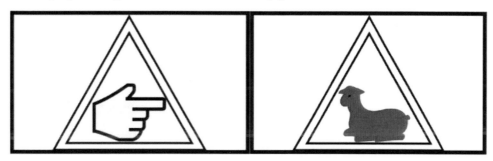

John the Baptist gave eyewitness testimony to what he had seen and heard, and he backed it up with the witness of Scripture. He laid this truth before the court: this is who Jesus is. Could they handle the truth?

We are confronted with the same question. When presented with the evidence of who Jesus is, how will we respond? If it's the truth, can we handle it? Will we allow it to define us and dictate our purpose, or will we choose a different path?

For we did not follow cleverly devised myths when we made known to you the power and coming of our Lord Jesus Christ, but we were *eyewitnesses* of his majesty. For when he received honor and glory from God the Father, and the voice was borne to him by the Majestic Glory, "This is my beloved Son, with whom I am well pleased," *we ourselves heard* this very voice borne from heaven, for *we were with him* on the holy mountain.
2 Peter 1:16-18 (emphasis added)

Day Three: First Disciples—What Are You Seeking? (John 1:35-51)

I really enjoy meeting new people because people fascinate me. There appears to be no end to stories of courage, coincidence, love, loss, heartbreak, and hope, and I love to hear them all. There's nothing wrong with a bit of healthy curiosity, but, unfortunately for the new people I meet, my curiosity can be a bit intense. I have the ability to ask a shocking number of questions in a very short span of time. Sometimes, after the dust has settled, I look back over the conversation and cringe because for the other person it probably felt more like an interrogation.

We're in the middle of a week of firsts. The first witness has been called to the stand. The first pieces of corroborating evidence have been presented. Tomorrow we'll see the first sign done by Jesus. In our passage today, we read about the first disciples being called. Five men from diverse backgrounds and socioeconomic statuses encounter Jesus, and each one of them comes to Jesus in a slightly different way. In this passage of first meetings, we'll encounter a lot of questions. Let's see the individual ways the first disciples come to Jesus and the questions which arise.

1. Read John 1:35-51.
    a. How did the first two disciples come to Jesus? (verses 35-37)

    b. Who was the third disciple to come to Jesus and how did his following come about? (verses 40-42)

    c. How did Philip, the fourth disciple, begin to follow Jesus? (verse 43)

    d. How did the fifth disciple, Nathanael, come to Jesus? (verses 45-46)

It might not be customary to conduct an interrogation on a first encounter, but it is common to ask questions when you're first getting to know someone. For these five men meeting Jesus, the same was true. Our passage of study today is sixteen verses long, and if you're doing your homework from the ESV Bible, you might have noticed five questions in these verses.

2. Each of the references below contains a question. Beside each one, jot down the question being asked, who is asking it, and — here you'll have to speculate somewhat, but do your best, using the evidence surrounding the question — what you think is the reason for asking it.

    a. Verse 38

    b. Verse 38

    c. Verse 46

    d. Verse 48

    e. Verse 50 (worded as a statement in the NIV Bible)

3. As you answered the first two questions, you may have noticed a repeated phrase. The phrase, or a variation of it, is spoken five times. Looking at verses 39, 46, 48, 50, and 51, what is the phrase?

4. Who or what is at the heart of this invitation to come and see?

5. We're going through this passage with a fine-toothed comb (the best way to begin study of the Bible). You came across a lot of different titles for, or ways of, referring to Jesus. Nine, in fact. Find them and write them down.

When the first two disciples turned from following John the Baptist to following Jesus, Jesus asked them what they were seeking. Were they seeking only a teacher? Were they seeking a king? Were they seeking the fulfillment of the Scriptures? And if so, why? So they could have national pride and prominence restored? Were they seeking a better life for themselves and their families? Having decided to follow Jesus, they knew they had found something — something new, something better. But did they fully know what they had chosen?

Throughout the Gospel of John, we will see examples of people who make profound statements with only limited understanding. Yesterday John the Baptist proclaimed Jesus as the Lamb of God. Did he know the fullness of his words? Not likely.

Looking ahead in John's Gospel, we read in John 11:49-52 that the high priest, Caiaphas, said it was better for one man to die for the people than to have the whole nation perish. Did he know the fullness of his words? Not even close!

The disciples stepped out in faith to follow Jesus when they still had only limited understanding. They knew they were seeking. They knew He was the answer to their questions. But there was still much they did not know.

The first chapter of John's Gospel ends with the first of twenty-five "Truly, truly" statements made by Jesus. Every time we come across this statement, we'll see that it is used by Jesus to draw attention to a particularly important point — a point He wants to emphasize as authoritative and truthful.

6. Write down the statement Jesus makes in verse 51.

If you're familiar with the Bible, you immediately see an Old Testament reference in Jesus' words. But if you're new to the Bible, you might wonder what Jesus is saying and why it's significant. We already know Jesus has attached great importance to this statement, so we need to find out why.

In Genesis, we encounter a man named Jacob. He's the son of Isaac, who was the son of Abraham, the man who first received the promises of God. Jacob was actually the second-born son of Isaac. He was not first in the line to inherit, but he lied to his dad and stole the inheritance from his older brother. Understandably, his older brother was livid, so Jacob was forced to flee for his life.

7. We'll pick up the story with Jacob fleeing. Read Genesis 28:10-17.
   a. What does Jacob see in his dream?

   b. Who stands above the scene in his dream?

   c. What does Jacob exclaim when he awakes?

   d. How does Jacob describe this place at the end of verse 17?

8. Having read the passage Jesus refers to, what do you think is the significant point that Jesus is making in John 1:51?

Today we read the witness of Jesus. He declares with authority that wherever He is, that is the house of God. He is the gate to heaven; the access to God.

And beginning with Moses and all the Prophets, [Jesus] interpreted to them in all the Scriptures the things concerning himself. Luke 24:27

Jesus is telling His first disciples, the men who would learn from Him throughout His entire earthly ministry, that He is Jacob's Ladder. The Scriptures they know and refer to easily, point to Him.

What the people saw but didn't recognize, the Word spoke clearly to illuminate. In our reading today, we kept bumping into the phrase, "You will see." That is why Jesus came to earth. To make a God who couldn't be seen, visible. To make Him known. So Jesus issues the invitation to come and see. He promises that if we follow Him with open eyes, open ears, and open hearts, we will see. As we spend our time in John's Gospel, let's pray our eyes will be open to see so that we can declare: I was lost but now am found; I was blind but now I see.

Blessed are your eyes, for they see . . . Matthew 13:16

Day Four: First Sign—You Will See Even Greater Things! (John 2:1-11)

I have attended many weddings. Throughout high school I often turned pages for a friend who was an accomplished pianist. If he wasn't available to play piano, people would sometimes settle for asking me to play for their wedding.

Being in the ceremony meant I was able to witness behind-the-scenes planning. I saw starry-eyed brides looking for songs that conveyed their feelings of undying love. I saw them strategically choose a venue that would set the tone for the rest of their lives—rustic, traditional, contemporary, off the beaten track. I saw them assemble a group of attendants, settle on décor, and perfect a menu. All this work had the same end goal: that the day would be perfect!

I can't tell you how many days did not live up to that expectation. I have been at outdoor weddings where the cacophony of birds drowned out the carefully-planned ceremony. I have seen brides in tears over decorations or dresses they dreamed would be beautiful enough to end up on the pages of a magazine but, in reality, fell far short of expectations.

If you're married, you can probably relate. Expectations run as high as emotions do at weddings, especially when the execution of the dream doesn't go as planned. We can laugh about it later when we tell our stories, but that doesn't stop future brides from dreaming, or planning, or from being upset when plans and dreams fall short. Rightly so, because weddings are a big deal. They are the joyous celebration of a new beginning.

We've been immersed in firsts this week. In the introductory teaching session, we saw that the prologue of John's Gospel pointed to the beginning of all things, but also to the beginning of a new thing. It's fitting then, that Jesus' first sign takes place at a wedding—a celebration of beginning.

1. Read John 2:1-11.
    a. Who do we see in attendance at the wedding in the first two verses?

    b. What serious problem emerges in verse 3?

c. Who brings this problem to Jesus' attention?

d. How does Jesus respond?

e. What is Mary's response to Jesus' words?

f. How is the problem resolved?

g. What does the master of the feast say to the bridegroom in verse ten? (In particular, the last sentence.)

h. For what purpose does Jesus perform this miracle, according to verse 11?

i. How do His disciples respond?

How did Jesus' response to His mother sit with you? You may have reacted to Him addressing her with the word "woman," but know that in that time and place it would not have been considered rude or derogatory. It did not indicate a lack of affection, but it did signal a rebuke.

2. Look more closely at John 2:4.
    a. What reason does Jesus give for not wanting to be involved?

    b. Look at John 7:30 and 8:20. Then look at John 12:23-27 and 13:1. What do you think Jesus meant by the phrase?

    c. What do you think was the meaning behind Jesus' rebuke?

When Jesus' parents presented Him in the temple, the prophet Simeon spoke specifically to Mary, Jesus' mother, to tell her that a sword would pierce her soul. (Luke 2:35) How hard those words must have been for a new mother to hear! Though Mary was to be Jesus' earthly mother, her Son was given from heaven for heaven's purpose. As God's sent Son, He was on God's timetable, not man's. Though He was part of an earthly family for a short period of time, we saw in John 1:12 that He came to offer all people the opportunity to become part of His eternal family.

The only way into this family is through believing that He is not simply Jesus of Nazareth, son of Mary and Joseph. He is Jesus the Messiah, Son of God. There are no special privileges of entry for anyone. But there are also no restrictions for anyone who comes to Him.

For every mother who has raised, nurtured, and loved a child, wouldn't it feel like a sword to the heart to know that, while your child does not esteem you less than others, they do not esteem you more?

3. Do you think Mary's response in verse five indicates a response of faith? Why or why not?

We now come to the problem Mary identified. There was no wine. This was a wedding. A joyful celebration of new beginnings and the celebration ran dry. We've already seen John point his readers to the dryness of the time. Jesus came to people in darkness. He came to His own, but they didn't receive Him. The voice that went before Him to prepare His way cried out in the wilderness rather than the temple, and this voice told the people that there was One among them that they didn't know. Jesus Christ, the Son of God had come. He was the Wellspring of Life for their parched and dry land. He was Living Water who alone could satisfy every soul. He was the New Beginning in whom all could find life.

4. Beside the following references, jot down the impact Jesus' coming had on this dark and dry land.
    a. John 1:5

    b. John 1:12

    c. John 1:16

    d. John 1:29

5. This is going to take a bit of math, but approximately how much wine resulted from the first sign?

6. What quality was the wine?

Signs are significant for what they point to. No one plans, prepares, and saves up for a family trip to Disneyland only to take pictures beside the sign, then turn around and go back home. You're not going for the sign, you're going for what it represents. The sign is pretty. But the fun — the party — is past the gates.

The wine wasn't the point — it was the symbol pointing to the real party.

7. Read Jeremiah 31:10-14.
    a. Along with the grain and the oil, what does the wine represent?

    b. What are some words in this passage that represent the joyous *quality* of what God is doing?

    c. What are some words/phrases that indicate the *quantity* of what He is doing?

The old wine had run out. Jesus told the servants to take the stone jars for the Jewish rites of purification and to fill them to the brim. Then He turned the contents of those jars into something new and better, because a new beginning had come for all of history. God, Himself, had come down.

Some of the people at the wedding did not know where this new wine had come from. But those closest to Him — those wanting to see — saw that this sign manifested Jesus' glory. And they believed.

Therefore, if anyone is in Christ, he is a new creation. The old has passed away; behold the new has come. 2 Corinthians 5:17

Day Five: Personal Reflection

Today is a day for personal reflection and application—a personal time between you and God. Pick one or two of the questions below, and journal, pray, or reflect on them. The best way to start is by asking how God is revealed in the passage. Then respond—what is true about you or your situation in light of who God has revealed Himself to be?

1. **John 1:29-31 The next day John saw Jesus coming toward him and said, "Look, the Lamb of God, who takes away the sin of the world! This is the one I meant when I said, 'A man who comes after me has surpassed me because he was before me.' I myself did not know him, but the reason I came baptizing with water was that he might be revealed to Israel."**

   After reading about the significance of the lamb in Israel's history, then hearing John refer to Jesus as "the Lamb of God," how does this name for Jesus speak to you in new ways?

2. **John 1:51 [Jesus said} "I tell you the truth, you shall see heaven open, and the angels of God ascending and descending on the Son of Man."**

   Genesis 28:12-13, 16-17 [Jacob] had a dream in which he saw a stairway resting on the earth, with its top reaching to heaven, and the angels of God were ascending and descending on it. There above it stood the LORD...When Jacob awoke from his sleep, he thought, "Surely the LORD is in this place, and I was not aware of it...This is none other than the house of God; this is the gate of heaven."

   Jesus declared with authority that wherever He is, that is the house of God. He is the gate to heaven, the access to God. How does your heart respond when you reflect on the truth of His statement?

3. **John 1:5 The light shines in the darkness but the darkness has not overcome it.**
   John 1:12 Yet to all who received him, to those who believed in his name, he gave the right to become children of God.
   John 1:16 From the fullness of his grace we have all received one blessing after another.
   John 1:29 "Look, the Lamb of God, who takes away the sin of the world!"

   Presented with evidence of who Jesus is, how will you respond?
   Will you allow this truth to define you and dictate your purpose, or will you seek a different path?

Teaching Session Two: Jesus Cleanses the Temple (John 2:12-22)

❖ All God's interactions with His people through the Old Covenant had prepared them for their Messiah and taught them how He would interact with them in the New Covenant.
  ◆ All the signs from the Old Testament, followed correctly, led to Jesus.

❖ The Feast of Passover was the most important event on the Jewish calendar. For the Jewish people it was associated with judgement and deliverance: judgement for those who didn't believe God's word so didn't seek safety under the blood of a lamb, and deliverance for those who believed and sought safety under the blood of a lamb.
  ◆ God had instructed His people to observe the Passover at the place He chose for His name to dwell (Deuteronomy 16:2).
  ◆ The place where Passover was remembered carried as much significance as the feast itself, because this was the place God met with His people.

❖ The tabernacle was the place where God's people had seen tangible evidence of His presence among them. (This structure was God's dwelling place among His people until Solomon built the temple—a more permanent dwelling place.)
  ◆ God's people turned their back on Him, they were taken into exile, and the magnificent temple was ransacked and burned by the Babylonians. (2 Chronicles 36:18-19)
  ◆ The people repented so God made a way of return. The temple was rebuilt, but this one didn't have the glory of the first and never witnessed a visible manifestation of God's presence.

❖ The temple in Jerusalem was empty of what it needed most, but it wasn't empty. It was Passover and business was booming.
  ◆ The busyness of business pulled worshipper's attention away from the real reason they were there.
  ◆ Their worship was distracted and distorted, and it was also dirtied by discrimination.

The temple was to be the meeting place between God and His people, but it was also to be the place God would meet with all people.

❖ The outermost area of the temple grounds was the Court of the Gentiles. Warning signs posted on pillars separated this court from the rest of the temple and cautioned any non-Jew that going beyond this point would result in death.
  ◆ All of the buying and selling was happening in the Court of the Gentiles. It wasn't Jewish worship that was being disrupted, it was Gentile worship.

- ❖ What fueled Jesus' anger?
  - ♦ Gentiles were supposed to hear of God's great Name and His mighty acts. They were supposed to come to His house to seek Him, and God's plan had always been that they, too, would be heard. (1 Kings 8:41-43, Isaiah 56:1, 3-8)
  - ♦ The religious leaders, those on the inside, were unconcerned about the spiritual state of the outsiders. They were more concerned that it be *their* temple and *their* worship rather than a house of joyful prayer for all people.

- ❖ Anything in our worship that distorts, or distracts, or discriminates in such a way that people cannot see God clearly, needs to be tossed. The attitude of us versus them, insider versus outsider, should be unheard of among God's people.

- ❖ God was doing a new thing through Jesus and there would no longer be a physical meeting place between God and man. Jesus is the meeting place. He is the ladder of access and wherever He is, that is the house of God.
  - ♦ When this dwelling place was broken and destroyed through death, it would be raised again, not to be another physical dwelling place but a spiritual one. This temple of Jesus' body had to be destroyed so that He could become the meeting place, not just for the Jewish people, but for all people.

But Jesus on his part did not entrust himself to them, because he knew all people and needed no one to bear witness about man, for he himself know what was in man. John 2:24-25

- ❖ Jesus knows what is in the hearts of us all. He isn't interested in labels. He's interested in hearts. He wants to cleanse our hearts from the distraction, the distortion, and the discrimination that dirties our worship.

Session Notes:

WEEK TWO: WHAT'S ON THE INSIDE?

In our last teaching session together, we witnessed the first confrontation between Jesus and the religious leaders. It occurred during the most significant religious feast of the Jewish year, and at the location that represented the meeting place between God and mankind. Jesus went to the temple during the Feast of the Passover to do some cleaning up and cleaning out. He emptied it of the distortion, distraction, and discrimination that dirtied worship. Jesus got rid of the old because He was bringing in the new.

Jesus' first confrontation was with corporate-level religious activity. John's Gospel will now switch from a wide-angle lens on the culture at large to zoom in with sharp focus on the individual heart. This week we will see two very different encounters with Jesus. The first is initiated by a powerful leader of the Jews. The second is initiated by Jesus with an outsider.

The introduction to our week of study is found in John 2:24-25. Jesus doesn't need anyone to tell Him what is in a person's heart. He sees hearts.

As we encounter Jesus in the Word this week, He encounters us. Pray that as our response to Him reveals our heart, we will have faith to step out, trusting His life-giving light.

No one has ever seen God; the only God, who is at the Father's side, he has made him known.
John 1:18

Day One: A Ruler of the Jews (John 3:1-12)

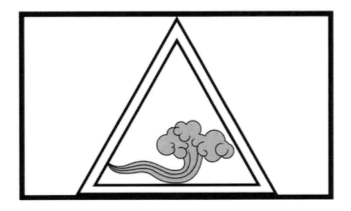

Jesus on his part did not entrust himself to them, because he knew all people and needed no one to bear witness about man, for he himself knew what was in man.
Now there was a man of the Pharisees named Nicodemus, a ruler of the Jews. John 2:24-25; 3:1

I love how, with just a couple of sentences, John sets the scene for the first individual encounter with Jesus. We're probably not surprised at the kind of person who pops up on the scene. It's a Pharisee. And not just any mid-level Pharisee, but rather a member of the Sanhedrin—one of the ruling class, the elite. Nicodemus had a position of power.

Big surprise, right? Powerful people have access. We see it all the time with celebrities, world leaders, the rich, the movers and shakers. Not much is off limits to them. So maybe we read the first verse of John chapter three and roll our eyes, muttering cynically, *of course **he** has access to Jesus.* We might even be tempted to flip the page to another story instead of stopping to read this one. Please don't, because the surprise of the story is not that Nicodemus had access to Jesus, it's how Jesus responds to him.

When Rome made Judea a province in A.D. 6, they gave the Sanhedrin, a group of Sadducees and Pharisees headquartered in Jerusalem, the power to handle internal Jewish affairs. Nicodemus was both a Pharisee and a member of the Sanhedrin.

The role of the Pharisees was to interpret the Law of God for the people, clarifying how it should be followed in daily life. In this way they controlled many aspects of everyday life for Jewish people. Pharisees decided what could or couldn't be done and they had the power to discipline people who didn't live up to their standards. Righteousness—right living—was everything to them.

Unlike the Sadducees, the Pharisees believed in the resurrection of the dead, so they believed that all their right living would be rewarded by a warm welcome into the Kingdom of God when their life on earth ended. They believed all Jews, except those who denied the faith, would inherit the kingdom of God as a privilege of natural birth. So the job of a Pharisee was to ensure that those who were born Jews would live like Jews until they died as Jews, so they could enter the Kingdom of the God who chose the Jews. Within an already privileged group of chosen people, Nicodemus was the most privileged of all. And he believed that as it was on earth, it would be in heaven.

1. With this background, read John 3:1-12 through once, then go back to the beginning of the passage and read more carefully to catch what is being said.
    a. When does Nicodemus come to Jesus?

    b. Check out other times John uses the term "night" in his Gospel in John 9:4; 11:10; and 13:30. When you consider that the author has introduced this encounter by saying Jesus knew what was in the heart of mankind, what do you think is being implied in John 3:2 by referring to the time?

    c. Write down the statement that Nicodemus opens with in verse 2. What does he say they know?

    d. Does it surprise you that a powerful religious leader comes to Jesus with a statement rather than a question? Why or why not? What do you think is the significance of this?

    e. Who do you think Nicodemus meant by "we" in his statement?

    f. What proof does Nicodemus use for making this statement? (Find this by looking for a word that indicates cause such as "because" or "for.")

Do you get the sense that Nicodemus is coming to Jesus in arrogance? Do you wonder if, just maybe, he felt like Jesus should be impressed that He had access to Nicodemus rather than Nicodemus feeling privileged that he had access to Jesus? We don't know what is in the heart of another. Really we don't. We can guess at it or speculate about it, and often we do. But we will never fully understand what motive or background in their life story compels them to behave the way they do. For better or for worse, we look at others through eyes far too coloured by what is true of ourselves.

Thankfully this is not the case with Jesus. He knows what is in a man or a woman. He sees with perfect clarity the deepest and darkest things. Even when we think we're coming to Him under the cover of darkness, concealing what we don't want exposed, He will shine His light on it to make it known.

That's what Jesus does with Nicodemus. He doesn't mince words or skirt around the issue. Instead He responds to Nicodemus' statement with an emphatic one of His own. What He says must have almost knocked Nicodemus flat onto the floor.

2. What statement does Jesus make to Nicodemus in John 3:3? What is He saying?

Nicodemus' whole life—literally his minute-by-minute life—was consumed with living righteously so that he could someday see the Kingdom of God. He believed that because he was privileged to be born a Jew, the Kingdom of God was his birthright. He thought that because he lived like a Jew so well, the Kingdom of God was what he deserved.

Jesus looks him in the eye and says emphatically, "Truly, truly, I say to you." Singular 'you.' It's personal. Jesus tells Nicodemus that for him—and yes, for everyone—to see the kingdom of God, they have to be born again. Doesn't this sound the same as what Jesus said to His mother at the wedding in Cana? There's no privilege of birth for anyone.

The physical context of your birth does not define you spiritually; not for better and not for worse.

Nicodemus came to Jesus with a statement not a question. He thinks he has answers. But Jesus turns the conversation on its head.

This is the point where Nicodemus starts sputtering questions. And they're not great are they? Nicodemus asks Jesus if He expects people to undergo what they both know is a physical impossibility. Jesus responds by saying *you're getting the physical and the spiritual mixed up.*

3. Refer to John 3:5-10.
   a. With what phrase does Jesus begin His response to Nicodemus in verse five and what does it imply?

   b. What does Jesus say to Nicodemus in verse seven?

   c. What reason does Jesus give to support His expectation that Nicodemus should understand what is being said to him? (verse 10)

Reading Jesus' answer about water, wind, and spirit in our modern context might have us empathizing with Nicodemus' trouble to understand. But it's pretty clear that Jesus expected a teacher of Israel to understand what He was saying. It was their job to know the Scriptures.

Nicodemus was familiar with the writings of the Jewish prophets. He knew many of the prophets looked forward to a time when the spirit would be poured out on all people. He probably could have spouted more than a dozen references off the top of his head to support this idea.

But the reference that likely shouted loudest of all was from the prophet Ezekiel.

4. Read Ezekiel 36:24-27.
    a. What does God say He will do in verse 24?

    b. What does He say He will do in verse 25 and why will He do it?

    c. What will He do next in verse 26?

    d. What will He do in verse 27 and what will be the purpose of doing it?

    e. Based on what Jesus said to Nicodemus that night, what is the personal implication of these verses for Nicodemus?

Nicodemus, a righteous ruler of the chosen people, is told by the man he'd declared was from God—the man he'd said God was with—that he would not be able to participate in the Kingdom of God unless He was cleansed from his uncleanness and idolatry.

The man whose whole life was centred around preserving ritual purity and cleanliness was unclean? The man who interpreted and enforced the Laws of the only God needed to be washed clean of the idolatry that clung to him? He needed a new heart? That which is alive does not need to be re-born, but Jesus told Nicodemus he needed a new birth. Nicodemus knows that though he has not associated with death or dead things because they are unclean, Jesus is telling him that he is spiritually dead!

Jesus tells Nicodemus that the wind of the Spirit, though unseen, can accomplish what seems like an impossibility. Nicodemus, a leader in Israel, confident in the Scriptures and their interpretation, responds to this statement of Jesus with the question, "How can this be?!"

The truth of the matter is, he knew how it could be—he just didn't like the implication of it! How did he know? Because he could have recited the creation account from Genesis by memory, telling how the breath of God entered Adam, changing him from a man of dust into a living being by the wind of the Spirit.

He knew how it could be because he was a Pharisee and believed in the resurrection of the dead. Every time the body of a faithful Jew was laid down into the rest of death, Nicodemus believed that those still and silent bones would one day breathe again. And do you know one of the passages of Scripture that underpinned that belief? Ezekiel 37, the passage that followed the one Jesus had just referred to.

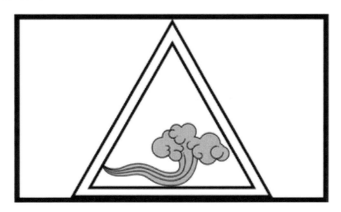

Nicodemus would have known the story of the valley of dry bones from Ezekiel 37 inside and out. He could have asked with Ezekiel, "Can these dry bones live?" He could have repeated the words the LORD told Ezekiel to prophesy over the bones, "O dry bones, hear the word of the LORD." And to those bones, dry and baking in the heat of the Middle Eastern sun, he could have spoken the word of the LORD, "Come from the four winds, O breath, and breathe on these slain, that they may live." (Ezekiel 37:3, 4, 9)

He could have pictured the breath of an unseen wind raising up an army.

Nicodemus came to Jesus at night with a confident statement, "Rabbi, we know that you are a teacher come from God, for no one can do these signs that you do unless God is with him." And Jesus confronted him on every single point.

If you know I am a teacher, are you prepared to learn from me?
If you know I have come from God, do you not realize that I will also know the way back to God?
If you know I am doing signs, will you stop at the sign or will you journey to the place the sign points to?
If God is with me, then why don't you believe what God and I testify to?

Jesus shines a bright light on Nicodemus' heart and reveals that for Nicodemus it is not an issue of knowledge or understanding. He already has both. It's an issue of belief.

We will finish the encounter between Jesus and Nicodemus tomorrow. Today, let's wrestle alongside him.

What holds us back — a lack of knowledge or a lack of belief?

But when the goodness and loving kindness of God our Saviour appeared, he saved us, not because of works done by us in righteousness, but according to his own mercy, by the washing of regeneration and renewal of the Holy Spirit, whom he poured out on us richly through Jesus Christ our Saviour, so that being justified by his grace we might become heirs according to the hope of eternal life. Titus 3:4-7

Day Two: What's in a Man? (John 3:13-36)

Ignorance is bliss.

Is ignorance really bliss? I've said it a hundred times if I've said it once. I've said ignorance is bliss when I've found out what I didn't want to know and would be just as happy continuing to not know. I've lamented that ignorance is not bliss when I've discovered what I wished I had known sooner. Maybe the point of the saying is that when you don't know something, you can't be expected to act upon it — either positively or negatively. But once you have knowledge, it's expected to inform your action.

My husband will be the first to affirm that knowledge should inform action. As it relates to me, specifically, he'd say one area he'd like to see this lived out better would be in regards to the vehicle I drive. He has taken the time to explain the symbols that could appear on the dash. Having done this, he believes I will act appropriately, should they appear.

When I still lived in blissful ignorance, thinking the low tire pressure warning light was simply an exclamation point inside of a horseshoe (maybe a hearty good luck sign?), I could be excused for driving until there was no tire left, only rim. But after it'd been explained to me, more was expected of me.

I have proven slow to understand. Rob believes my slowness stems from either apathy where vehicle maintenance is concerned (I believe it's really someone else's problem), or from avoidance (knowing what the light represents means that when I see it, I know I'm facing time-consuming, costly action so I choose ignore it).

Yesterday we saw that Jesus did not allow Nicodemus to feign lack of knowledge or understanding as his barrier. He knew, he just didn't like what his knowledge implied. His knowledge implied action and cost to him.

When dealing with Nicodemus, Jesus didn't vaguely allude to the truth, hoping Nicodemus would come to an understanding of the gravity of the situation on his own. Jesus painted Nicodemus a picture that left no room for misinterpretation. Let's pick up where we left off yesterday.

1. Read John 3:9-15.

   a. Fill in the blanks from verse 14: "And as Moses lifted up the serpent in the wilderness, _____ must the Son of Man be lifted up that _____ who _____ in him may have eternal _____." (Use the NIV Bible. The blanks will be slightly different in the ESV.)

   b. Now turn to Numbers 21:4-9 and read the account of Moses and the serpent that Jesus refers to. What does God do in verse 6, in response to the Israelites' grumbling?

   c. What solution does He provide?

   d. Why do you think Jesus references this passage at this point in His conversation with Nicodemus? What is He telling Nicodemus?

   e. What solution does Jesus offer those who believe?

For the Israelites dying from the fiery serpent bites in the wilderness, neither avoiding the problem nor misdiagnosing the problem was a good idea. It led to death. Jesus had just told Nicodemus his spiritual condition was the same as the physical condition of those Israelites. But just as God offered the solution to physical death, Jesus offers the solution to spiritual death.

Those snake-bitten Israelites could know all about the healing power of the bronze snake Moses made and erected in their midst. But if they did not believe in it enough to lift their eyes up to it, their knowledge did them no good.

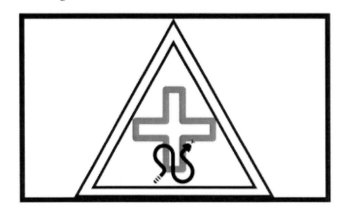

God knows the true impact that long-ago serpent bite had on humanity. The encounter with the serpent in the Garden brought death as surely as the serpents in the wilderness. God knew, so He acted.

2. Read John 3:16-17.
    a. What action did God take based on His knowledge of the true state of human hearts?

    b. Why did God act?

    c. For whom did God act?

    d. What is required of humanity in response to this act?

    e. What is the outcome for people who know, believe, and then respond?

Belief is more than a fuzzy feeling;
it is the confidence that someone or something is true, followed by action demonstrating this to be so.

God knew the certain outcome for us: death by sin. He acted. He acted in a way that proved what is true of Him. This is *how* He loved the world. This is how *much* He loved the world. He gave His one-of-a-kind Son.

God gave His Son to be lifted up like the bronze serpent in the wilderness, not as a punishment for sin, but as the antidote for sin.
The Son is the cure.

The identity of the Messiah is on trial. But once confronted with the truth claims of Jesus that He is the Messiah, a response is required from us. We flip from prosecutor to defendant and our response determines our outcome.

3. Read John 3:18-21.
    a. What is the outcome for those who do not believe the truth of Jesus' claim? (verse 18)

    b. What is the judgment (verdict) that is handed down? (verse 19)

c. What is the evidence used to support the judgment (verdict)? (verses 20-21)

d. What is the message or meaning behind Jesus' words here? What is He saying to Nicodemus?

4. Do you think a successfully religious person like Nicodemus would like the implication of John 3:21? Why or why not?

Maybe I was a little smug at the beginning of Jesus' encounter with Nicodemus. I kind of enjoyed seeing a powerful know-it-all get knocked down a peg or two. But that spotlight has shone on me, too, and I feel exposed by its brightness.

Apart from the redemptive work of Christ, I'm in the same boat as Nicodemus — spiritually dead and without the physical or spiritual capacity to save myself from eternal death. I've enjoyed privilege and have wanted to keep my social circle small and exclusive rather than open it up for everyone and anyone because I thought it was mine to control. I've enjoyed the darkness of pride in accomplishment; I want the credit because I believe I deserve it. I have enjoyed darkness — hidden in it, been comforted by it, and sought to hold onto it. Standing before the court of public opinion, I have felt confident.

Standing before the Judge of all the earth, I see my guilty verdict.

As God's children in the wilderness felt the fiery bite of the serpents and called out to Him for rescue, I, too can lift my eyes and see my redemption. It is in the One who was lifted up on the cross of death and turned it into the Tree of Life.

Ignorance is not bliss. Bliss is knowing the true nature of my sin-dead heart and receiving the antidote for it. Bliss is acting on what I believe to be true, confident He will prove true.

But God shows his love for us in that while we were still sinners, Christ died for us.
Romans 5:8

5. What are some areas of darkness you see in your own life? In what ways are you holding on to those things, seeking comfort and security from them? Bring them before the cross by confessing them to the Father and exposing them to the light.

As we close today, let's shift our gaze from Nicodemus to John the Baptist. Another man born into privilege. His father was a priest. His mother was descended from the daughters of Aaron. This was a man set apart from before he was born to carry out an important mission. Luke's

Gospel records that an angel told his father, Zechariah, that many would rejoice at his son's birth because he would be great before the Lord, and that this child would grow and turn many of the people of Israel back to God. (Luke 1:15-16)

Can you imagine being told that about your son before he was born? Can you imagine growing up knowing this was true of you?

I believe one of the most beautiful glimpses of how this impacted John the Baptist is not found in the fact that he lived in the wilderness wearing camel skin and eating locusts. Some people are into camping enough that this just might be okay with them. I think one of the most humbling pictures of John's heart is recorded in the Gospel of John.

6. Read John 3:22-36. John the Baptist is busy doing exactly what he's been called to do. The prophecy of the angel has come true and he has disciples who are following him.
    a. And then what happens, according to verse 26?

    b. Summarize his response from verses 27-30.

John the Baptist has been told that people will listen to him and that his life will have influence, but he is content to remain great before the Lord rather than strive to be great before man.

God sees into hearts. We can trust Him to act rightly based on what He sees.

Nicodemus comes to Jesus in confidence and Jesus exposes the shaky foundations his confidence rests on. Nicodemus had heard the words of Jesus and the last we hear from him in this encounter, is the question/statement, "How can these things be?" After this there is only silence.

In Matthew 11 and Luke 7 we glimpse the end of John the Baptist's life. He's lived his life on mission from God, and now he's sitting in prison. But instead of confidence in a mission fulfilled, John the Baptist struggles with doubt. Was Jesus really the Messiah? Was his mission complete? John the Baptist had enough faith to take action. He made his doubt face the truth and sent some of his disciples to Jesus to ask if He was the one to come or if they should look for another. (Matthew 11:3; Luke 7:19) Seeing into John the Baptist's heart, Jesus does not condemn him for doubting. He commends John for his belief in front of the crowd who heard John's doubt.

What did you go out into the wilderness to see? A reed shaken by the wind? What then did you go out to see? A man dressed in soft clothing? Behold, those who are dressed in splendid clothing and live in luxury are in kings' courts. What then did you go out to see? A prophet? Yes, I tell you, and more than a prophet. This is he of whom it is written, 'Behold, I send my messenger before your face, who will prepare your way before you.' I tell you, among those born of women none is greater than John. Yet the one who is least in the kingdom of God is greater than he. Luke 7:24-28

Friends, our greatness in God's eyes is not based on what we've done or on how we're seen by others. It is in our response to His revelation of Himself. Do you live like this is true?

And the Word became flesh and dwelt among us, and we have seen his glory, glory as of the only Son from the Father, full of grace and truth. John 1:14

Day Three: Living Water (John 4:1-27)

With joy you will draw water from the wells of salvation. Isaiah 12:3

I have often lamented my impulsive nature. I'm prone to act before I have all the information. And I'm a go-big-or-go-home kind of girl, so my actions tend to be bigger than the situation warrants. When I try to slow myself down, I feel a bit like a preschool child sitting on her hands and biting her tongue during circle time.

Sometimes, when I'm headed in the direction of too much too fast, one of my sisters will say, "You don't have to move them into your house, maybe just invite them for supper." (She says this, because of the time I felt like I should move a large family I'd never met into our house because they were in a time of need. My sister advised that perhaps I invite them over for a meal first.) Even when my intentions are good, I'm not always clear on the best way to act on them.

This is partly why I've always loved the story of the woman at the well. I resonate with her. False starts and stumbles don't stop her from moving forward. When she doesn't understand everything, she trusts the importance of what she does understand enough to act on it. Let's get right into the story.

1. Read through John 4:1-27 first before stopping to answer the questions. It's a longer passage than we've had so far, but it reads like a fast moving story and the details are easy to follow.
    a. Where does the story take place? (General and specific location)

    b. At what time of day does it take place?

    c. Verse 7 introduces the two main characters. Who are they, and who initiates the encounter?

d. Good story arcs involve tension that needs to be resolved. What tension is revealed between the main characters in verse 9?

e. Write down similarities you see between this encounter and the one between Jesus and Nicodemus.

f. Write down differences you notice between the two encounters.

Jesus' encounter with Nicodemus takes place in the Jewish religious capital. His encounter with the woman takes place in the Roman province of Judea, but in the part of the province dominated by non-Jewish people — people the Jews viewed as unclean. Nicodemus came to Jesus at night; Jesus engaged the woman at the sun's highest point of the day. While Jesus and Nicodemus were both Jews (they had the same culture, knew the same Scriptures, had been raised in the same customs) Jesus and the woman were members of people groups that despised each other.

The reason for the hatred that existed between Jews and Samaritans began at the time of the Assyrian exile of the Northern Kingdom (Israel). We can read about it in 2 Kings 17:24-41. I'd love for you to turn there and read the story for yourself, so if you have the time, please do. But we've got a lot of ground to cover today so, in case you're pressed for time, I'll summarize what happened.

After conquering the region of Samaria, the king of Assyria exiled the who's who in this part of Northern Israel, leaving behind sparsely populated cities which he then re-populated by bringing in people from five other conquered nations to live with the Jewish survivors. Over time, the Israelites who stayed intermarried with the foreigners. This was a problem. Not a racial or cultural problem, rather it was a worship issue.

2. In Exodus 20:1-6, what did God command of the Israelites?

3. What was happening in Samaria that would have caused great tension between the law-abiding Jews and the Samaritans in 2 Kings 17:41?

Mixed in both ethnic background and religion, the people of Samaria had some of the Hebrew Scriptures — the first five books of the Hebrew Old Testament. In Deuteronomy 27:9-14, they read about Moses instructing the priests to pronounce blessings on the people from Mount Gerizim upon entering the Promised Land. Against Jewish custom, Samaritans believed this was the proper place to worship so they built a temple there around 400 BC. The Jews destroyed this temple almost 300 years later.

It is likely that Jesus and the Samaritan woman looked upon the temple ruins on Mount Gerizim as they spoke.

With this background in mind, let's dig a little deeper into our story in John.

4. What does Jesus do in verse 6 and why does He do it?

5. Why do you think the woman comes to the well in the heat of the day? What does this tell us about her social standing and maybe even about her self-worth?

6. What does Jesus do in verse 7 and what can we see were cultural restrictions around this behaviour from verse 27?

7. What does Jesus address in verses 16-18?

8. Re-read Jesus' words to Nicodemus in John 3:17. With this in mind, why do you think Jesus addresses this issue? What need is He exposing?

My heart constricts when I read that the One who was from heaven came to the earth He created and experienced human limitations like thirst and fatigue. I marvel that the One who is Jacob's ladder had to sit beside Jacob's well when He was weary. I'm humbled to read that when God came to His own people in the person of Jesus, He was treated like an outsider, yet He never saw anyone that way. For the sake of my eternal soul, I rejoice that the One who could condemn me for my sin, does not expose sin to shame, but only to heal.

Knowing the true state of her life and her heart before He ever sat down at that well, Jesus initiates an encounter with this woman because He wants to issue an invitation.

9. What two things does Jesus offer the Samaritan woman in verse 10?

10. Think about the character of the woman Jesus is addressing and what He is now offering her—a gift from God, Jesus, Himself. What does this offering reveal about who He is and why He has come? (Hint: see Matthew 9:12-13)

For God so loved the world, that he *gave* . . . (John 3:16)

If you knew the *gift* of God . . . (John 4:10)

11. In verse 21, Jesus tells the woman that where she worships is not the issue. Instead, he tells her she needs to know Who she worships. Jesus doesn't sugar coat His response in verse 22. What does He tell her?

When dealing with Nicodemus, Jesus quickly cut to the root of Nicodemus' sin. It wasn't lack of knowledge it was a lack of belief. He told Nicodemus that you can do all the right things but if you're doing them in your own strength and for your own purposes, you're wasting your time.

When dealing with this woman, Jesus again cuts to the root. Her problem was a lack of knowledge. He tells her you're doing the wrong things.

Worship that pleases God is not bound up in rituals of time and place but freely given from the heart in spirit and in truth. Not whatever truth we might create for ourselves but the truth revealed by and in the Word of God. To all seeking truth, Jesus extends this invitation:

Come, everyone who thirsts, come to the waters; and he who has no money, come, buy and eat! Come, buy wine and milk without money and without price.
Behold, I made him a witness to the people, a leader and commander for the peoples. Behold, you shall call a nation that you do not know, and a nation that did not know you shall run to you, because of the LORD your God, and of the Holy One of Israel, for he has glorified you. Seek the LORD while he may be found; call upon him while he is near; let the wicked forsake his way, and the unrighteous man his thoughts; let him return to the LORD, that he may have compassion on him, and to our God, for he will abundantly pardon. Isaiah 55:1, 4-7

To every person who has tried to create their own cistern only to watch it spring leaks and crack, Jesus says, *come*. To every person trying to plug holes and fix cracks by themselves, only to discover they can't keep up, Jesus says, *stop trying to make your creation work and trust that mine will*. To every person surrounded by pools of water that are fetid and stagnant, Jesus says, *come to living springs of fresh water.*

I am offering you a gift, and the gift is Me.

43

The woman's desire leaps off the page when she tells Jesus she knows the Messiah is coming and when he does, he'll explain everything. She doesn't understand yet, but she wants to.

Jesus looks a sinful, societal outcast in the eye and tells her that the One she is waiting for has arrived and that she's talking to Him. The wait is over.

Just then, the disciples come back. Jesus and the woman are interrupted, and so we, too, must wait for tomorrow to see how the story ends.

For with you is the fountain of life; in your light do we see light. Psalm 36:9

Day Four: The Saviour of the World (John 4:25-42)

We were at the climax of the story yesterday when we were interrupted.

The Samaritan woman had revealed that she was waiting for the Messiah to come and make things clear to her. Jesus told her He was the One she'd been waiting for. At this point, the disciples showed up on the scene and they were confused. What was Jesus doing talking to a woman? Engaging women in theological discussions was considered a waste of time by most men, potentially dangerous by others. But a Samaritan woman? That was way worse! Samaritan women were considered perpetually unclean.

For whatever reason (the Bible doesn't give it) the disciples don't verbalize their bewilderment when they see Jesus talking with an unclean woman. But their appearance on the scene interrupts the conversation and shifts the scene, nonetheless. Before switching his focus to Jesus and the disciples, John gives us one more over-the-shoulder glimpse of the woman.

1. Read John 4:25-42.
    a. What two things does the woman do after they're interrupted? (verse 28)

    b. What do you think these actions symbolize?

    c. What invitation does she extend in verse 29, and to whom does she extend it?

    d. Based on what Jesus revealed about her history, which wouldn't have been a secret to the townspeople, what significance do you see in the invitation she issues?

e. What question does she end verse 29 with, and what do you think she means by it?

f. How do her listeners respond? (verse 30)

In His encounter with Nicodemus, Jesus said this was the verdict: "The light has come into the world, and people loved the darkness rather than the light because their works were evil." (John 3:19) I like to tell my children to watch for big "buts" in the Bible because they point to very important truths. I say it in part because it makes them giggle, but more because I know it'll help them remember. Two verses after reading the verdict, we come to a big "but."

But whoever does what is true comes to the light. John 3:21

2. How does this verse relate to the Samaritan woman?

3. What does the woman's invitation in verse 29 reveal about her heart?

After giving us a glimpse of the Samaritan woman's exit from the scene, the author now turns our attention to Jesus' conversation with His disciples.

4. Read Deuteronomy 8:2-3. How do these verses help you understand what Jesus is saying to His disciples in John 4:31-34?

Jesus willingly submitted Himself to all the limitations of humanity. He knew physical need. But, being from heaven rather than earth, He knew that spiritual need far outweighed the physical.

5. According to John 6:39-40, what is the Father's will for the Son?

6. How does this tie into what Jesus is talking about in John 4:35-38?

7. You don't have to be a farmer to have a basic understanding of the order of operations and general timeline of how food grows.
   a. What difference does Jesus point out in the timeline between a physical harvest and a spiritual one? (verse 36)

b. According to verse 38, what has Jesus sent His disciples to do?

c. What does this reveal about God's will for each of us? List some practical ways you can sow and reap within the circles/communities God has placed you.

In the natural, physical order, there is a period of time between seeding and harvest. In the spiritual world, freshly sown seed can lead to an immediate harvest. The disciples were unsettled when they saw Jesus talking to a Samaritan woman, and probably felt relieved when she went away. But then she came back and she wasn't alone. The people of the Samaritan town were coming back with her.

The old was passing away. The new was being ushered in before their very eyes. They'd seen it when Jesus performed the first sign at the wedding in Cana. They saw it again when Jesus overthrew distorted religious activity at the temple. And when Jesus was confronted by a religious ruler who was ready to declare to the Teacher what he knew to be true, only to have it turned on its head, the disciples were probably there, too.

But still, having seen and heard so many signs that change was upon them, the disciples must have rubbed their eyes in wonder when they saw Jesus rejoicing over a harvest of souls led by a repentant sinner who was not only a Samaritan, but also a woman, low on knowledge and lower on morality.

A confident Nicodemus sputtered questions and disbelief, then retreated into the shadows when faced with the Light. A woman who'd been living in the shadow of darkness and sin felt the warmth of the Light when it shone on her and she stepped out into it. Desperately thirsty, she longed to drink from the well of salvation. And one life-giving sip was enough for her to know this water was too good to keep to herself. If this was a well she could drink from, there wasn't anyone who'd be turned away.

8. Refer to John 4:39-42.
   a. What was the initial reason the people in the Samaritan town believed?

   b. What was the reason their belief grew?

   c. Having heard for themselves, what conclusion did they come to?

   d. What encouragement do these verses give you to share your testimony? Explain.

We've seen Jesus looking into individual hearts this week in our homework. As we close, reflect on what God is revealing about your own heart. Does it feel empty like the ritual jars at the wedding, in need of the new wine of the spirit? Does your worship look like it's the right stuff at the right place, but in reality it's as false as the distorted, distracted, and discriminatory worship that was happening at the temple? Are you ready to step out into the light or will you still hide in the shadows, pretending that shades of black hide your figure?

God extends a gift – life through the light of His Son – and it's for everyone.

And we have seen and testify that the Father has sent his Son to be the Saviour of the world.
1 John 4:14

Day Five: Personal Reflection

Pick one or two of the questions below, and journal, pray, or reflect on them.

1. **The Message paraphrases Ezekiel 36:24-27 as follows: For here's what I'm going to do: I'm going to take you out of these countries, gather you from all over, and bring you back to your own land. I'll pour pure water over you and scrub you clean. I'll give you a new heart, put a new spirit in you. I'll remove the stone heart from your body and replace it with a heart that's God-willed, not self-willed. I'll put my Spirit in you and make it possible for you to do what I tell you and live by my commands.**

    In our homework, we considered the implication of these verses for Nicodemus; now consider their implication in your own life. Do you believe Jesus can make you clean or do you doubt this for yourself? Why or why not? Based on Jesus' interactions with Nicodemus and the Samaritan woman, what do you think a God-willed heart looks like? How does that translate to your own life?

2. **John 3:16-21 For God so loved the world, that he gave his only Son, that whoever believes in him should not perish but have eternal life. For God did not send his Son into the world to condemn the world, but in order that the world might be saved through him. Whoever believes in him is not condemned, but whoever does not believe is condemned already because he has not believed in the name of the only Son of God. And this is the judgment: the light has come into the world, and people loved the darkness rather than the light because their works were evil. For everyone who does wicked things hates the light and does not come to the light, lest his works should be exposed. But whoever does what is true comes to the light, so that it may be clearly seen that his works have been carried out in God.**

    Do these verses bring you comfort and hope or give you cause for concern? Are you walking in darkness or light? How do you know? How is the Lord leading you to respond?

3. This week we looked at the encounter between Jesus and Nicodemus (chapter 3) and Jesus and the Samaritan woman (chapter 4). One was an insider and the other an outsider—an outcast. What similarities with these two individuals do you see in yourself? Do you relate to one more than the other? Why? When Jesus shines His light in your life, what does He expose? How does He want you to respond?

Teaching Session Three: Inside, Outside, Wrong Side (John 4:43-54)

❖ Jesus is welcomed in Galilee. It had to have been exciting for the small town people of Galilee to have their local celebrity back in town—even if there was some notoriety attached to Him.

❖ Who turns up to encounter Jesus?
  ♦ A man not only on the outside but the wrong side—he worked for the power that oppressed the Jews.

  ♦ What was he doing there? Surely the Messiah couldn't be for him.

  ♦ What do you think it would have taken for a man with his position of power to come to someone who would have been seen as a small-town, backwoods yokel, and ask for help?

Unless you see signs and wonders you will not believe. John 4:48

❖ There's nothing wrong with enjoying the signs—as long as you see what the signs point to.

The man took Jesus at His word and departed. John 4:50

❖ What if we lived like what Jesus said was true and we allowed His words to change our lives?

View this teaching session at www.unshakenministries.com

❖ We are not called to blind faith, but to a well-informed faith which is driven by deep love. Sometimes, this kind of faith looks like having just enough faith to take the next step at His word.

❖ Jesus encountered and engaged both Nicodemus and the Samaritan woman and then He challenged them to confront the obstacles they each faced in coming to Him. They faced different obstacles because they were different people from different backgrounds.

❖ Seeing the signs comes with an implication of action based on what the signs point to.

❖ When we encounter God, we are confronted in the very areas we think we know, the areas we think we can't change, shouldn't change, or don't want to change. Encountering the Light of the World uncovers what we'd like to hide in darkness.

❖ Many of those He encountered were eagerly awaiting the promised King, the Messiah, their Deliverer. And yet, those same individuals chose to ignore the signs and turn their back on the very One who came to save.

❖ We are all guilty of missing the signs and their significance. We have all clung tightly to things we haven't wanted to lose hold of. And, we have all hid from the light, wanting to remain under the cover of darkness.

❖ Confrontation always comes with the Good News that God has come in the person of His Son, Jesus, with an invitation: this is who I am. All who come to know and believe that He is who He says He is, have open access to God and eternal life in His name.

Session Notes:

WEEK THREE: YOU'D RATHER HAVE MOSES?

The Word who spoke Creation into being was among them in the flesh. Jacob's ladder of open access between heaven and earth had arrived. The abundant grain and wine of the new covenant flowed. The One who was the temple had come. Jewish Scripture was being fulfilled.

Yet, in a shocking twist, we saw in our last teaching session that a Gentile soldier testified against God's people. In desperate need, this soldier went to Jesus. With only the assurance of Jesus' words, the man left in faith, trusting that what Jesus had said would be so. What a contrast to those who'd been entrusted with the Word, yet asked for signs and wonders.

When Jesus came to set His people free from the burden of a law they couldn't keep, they decided they'd rather have the law. When He told them the Scripture pointed to Him and He stood among them in fulfillment of it, they decided they were happier with the Scriptures. When He performed signs and wonders greater than anything they or their forefathers had ever seen, they asked Him to do more.

The One that Moses had been pointing to was among them, and they decided they'd rather have Moses.

There was a man sent from God, whose name was John. He came as a witness, to bear witness about the light, that all might believe through him. He was not the light, but came to bear witness about the light.
John 1:6-8

Day One: The Healing at the Pool (John 5:1-15)

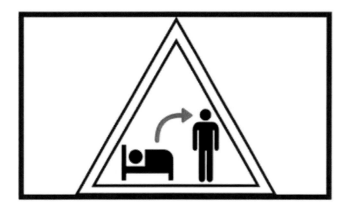

I have called Calgary home for decades and I am happy to do so. It's a fun place to live year-round, but each year in early July, the fun gets ramped up to a whole new level.

Every year our city hosts the greatest outdoor show on earth: The Calgary Stampede. Calgarians throw fashion sense out the window and clad themselves in denim and plaid. They don hats, buckles, and boots, to welcome visitors from all over the world.

For two weeks, Calgary is turned on its head. An increase in population combined with out-of-towners unfamiliar with our streets leads to significant congestion on major routes. Free pancake breakfasts scattered throughout the city every day of Stampede has even those who normally fear refined carbohydrates and saturated fats schedule two full weeks around these breakfasts, leading to a different kind of congestion.

Though the farthest reaches of the city are painted with Stampede fever, if you really want to feel the heat, you'll head downtown to the site of the Stampede Grounds. In this hotspot of activity, visitors can be entertained for days without ever laying eyes on the cattle and horses the Stampede is known for.

Should you be in our fair city during Stampede, the way you experience it will depend, to some degree, on your means. If money is something you have extra of, you'll pay the entrance fee to get past the gates and go on to enjoy your day eating, drinking, and being entertained to your heart's content. The fact that you pay more for a deep fried chocolate bar than you'd normally pay for an entire meal is not a concern.

Some people can't resist the lure of fun and excitement, but they lack the resources to simply let money flow. They pay the entrance fee to be allowed in, but carry backpacks stuffed with water and food, only paying for what they judiciously decide is worth the price.

And then there are those who'd never consider shelling out money for the food and the fun inside, because they don't even have the money to get past the gates. They might be where the party is at, but they can't pay the fee to get in.

Ever felt that way?

Let's turn to the fifth chapter of John. It tells the story of a man who knew this feeling all too well.

1. Read John 5:1-5.
   a. Where is this story taking place, both generally and then more specifically?

   b. Why was Jesus in Jerusalem and what do you think the atmosphere of the city might have been like at this particular time?

   c. How does John describe the crowd gathered around the pool?

   d. Look at the title of this passage: what does it tell us about why the people were there, and what were they waiting or hoping for?

   e. Who specifically is described in verse 5?

2. Now read John 5:6-9a.
   a. Who arrives on the scene next, and what does he know? (verse 6)

   b. What question does Jesus ask?

   c. Reread the answer in verse 7, look past the words themselves. What is the man expressing with his answer?

   d. How does Jesus respond?

   e. What is the result according to verse 9a, and in what time frame?

When I think of Jerusalem during a Jewish feast, I think of Calgary during Stampede. Noisy. Crowded. Party for some, salt in the wound for others. For nearly four decades the man in today's story lay impotent on the edge of the party.

This man was by the pool called Bethesda—house of mercy—and he must have known, heard of, or maybe even seen with his own eyes, someone who was healed here. Right? If no one had ever been healed in those waters, the sick and needy wouldn't have been attracted to them. But there they lay, clinging to hope.

We don't know if this man remained where he was because he clung to a thread of hope or because he simply didn't have the ability to be anywhere else. But there he was.

3. Who is the initiator of his rescue? (verse 6)

4. Flip back to John 1:1-5.
    a. What does verse 1 tell us about the Word?

    b. What does verse 3 tell us about Jesus' role in creation?

    c. According to verse 4, what does Jesus offer?

    d. What connection do you see between this verse and our story today?

In this man's mind, his best-case scenario was that someone would help him to the waters at exactly the right time, and just maybe he could be healed. He'd probably dreamt of a new life, a better life, where he was free from what bound him. But his dreams fell short. This man was looking only at the physical. But another Man, the One who sees hearts and meets needs, saw that this man needed something more.

Jesus shows up, seeks him out, and speaks. Just like so many times before, Jesus turns the social order of the day on its head. He points out the value of the individual, no matter their condition. He reveals God's love for all people, no matter how lovable they might be. Jesus offers life to all who will believe. All that Jesus is, He makes available to whoever will look to Him in their need.

Jesus simply spoke, and instantly the man was healed. Whether the man went on to receive the spiritual life Jesus offered is unclear, but we do know that his physical life was changed forever because of his encounter with the Son.

As you read and respond to this encounter, do you get the uneasy feeling that Jesus is asking you the same questions He asked the man by the pool?

Do you want to get well? Will you receive the life I offer? Will your life look different because of Me? Will you let go of the familiar to follow Me?

5. Is there something you sense God is asking of you today?

    a. Have you been resistant to His leading before today? Explain.

    b. How could you respond in obedience to Him?

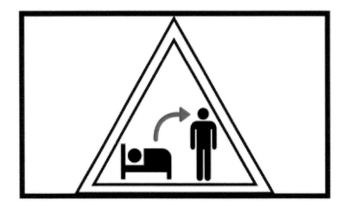

Pick up where you left off and read the rest of the story in John 5:9b-17.

6. How do the Jews respond to this event according to verse 10, and why do they respond this way?

7. How does the man who has been healed respond to the Jews in verse 11?

8. Jesus finds the healed man once again, and says something to him. With your background information from the story of Nicodemus and the Samaritan woman, what do you think Jesus is saying to this man in verse 14?

9. What does the man do in response, according to verse 15?

Honestly, I'm disappointed with the man in this story. He's in an impossible situation and experiences a miraculous delivery from it, but he couldn't be bothered to find out anything about his rescuer. Not even a name. When his rescuer seeks him out again, this time to intervene in his spiritual condition rather than his physical one, the only response we see from the man is that he goes and tells the Jewish leaders that he now knows who healed him. He ratted Jesus out. He got the gift, but he wasn't super interested in the giver.

Is it possible I'm critical of him because his attitude and actions shine a light on me?

All in all, this seems like a simple story, doesn't it? The man who had always been on the outside of the party looking in had his entrance fee paid. Not only could he get past the gates, he was offered fistfuls of spending money to take with him. But he doesn't seem grateful or changed. I'd like to think that if that were me, I'd be dancing through the gates and dragging my rescuer along so we could enjoy the party together. But the invitation is for me, too. The same offer is extended to me and to you: life in Him for eternity and joy in Him on the journey. I, like the man at the pool, have received the gift offered. I've been amazed by it, even. Yet, often, my response has sadly looked less like the response of the Samaritan woman, and more like the response of this man. I've looked past the Giver and only seen the gift. I've gone away thinking it was enough.

Whether we like the guy or not, he was the one Jesus sought out. He was the recipient of both grace and truth, and his experience with Jesus is another sign pointing to who Jesus is: the giver of life.

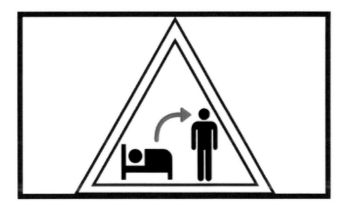

We are ready to wrap up today. But, before we do, I've got to say, there is something about the way John throws verse 9b into the mix, that I can't get out of my mind.

10. What does John point out in this verse?

11. What do you think Jesus' motive is for healing on the Sabbath? What message do you think He might have been sending?

Why on earth, would the Word, the One who was with God at the beginning, the One who spoke all that exists into being, and the One who was God Himself, have healed this man on the Sabbath?

It's almost as if the sign had less to do with the man and more to do with Jesus. It's almost like Jesus knew what day it was and purposely chose to reverse life-long impotency on the Sabbath in order to make a statement . . .

Jesus again said to them . . . I came that they may have life and have it abundantly.
John 10:10b

And [Jesus] said to them, "The Sabbath was made for man, not man for the Sabbath. So the Son of Man is lord even of the Sabbath." Mark 2:27-28

Day Two: Equal with God? (John 5:16-47)

So did he?!

Yesterday I said it was almost like Jesus chose to heal on the Sabbath to make a point? Did he?

1. Read John 5:16-18.
    a. Why were the Jews persecuting Jesus, according to verse 16?

    b. How does Jesus respond to them in verse 17?

    c. What is the big deal about Jesus' response, according to verse 18?

This is significant, so let's look at it a little closer.

2. Make a point-form list of all the things that God could potentially be doing on the Sabbath that would be considered work to the religious Jews.

I don't know what made it on your list, but I know that my oldest child was born on a Sunday. If that is considered the Sabbath, that moment, along with the births of all my children, is the most beautiful work of creation I have ever beheld. I know people who have passed from this life on a Sabbath. Based on Scripture, I am certain God was with them every moment of the transition to joyfully welcome them and settle them into their new home. I need only glance out my window at God's beautiful creation to know that He is actively sustaining it every moment of every day.

Religious Jews also had made lists of what could be done on the Sabbath and what could not. Some of the things that were forbidden included carrying anything from one domain to another, lifting anything beyond a certain weight, and lifting anything higher than your head.

Jewish Rabbis only needed to look at their world to make the same observations you and I just did. They could see God was always at work, sustaining His creation. In an effort to understand how it was okay for God to do what could be considered breaking His own rules, they came to the conclusion that God working on the Sabbath was not a violation of His own command of Sabbath rest, because all of creation is His. Nothing He could carry would be carried outside of His domain, and nothing He could lift could be lifted higher than Him. (Carson D. , 1991)[1]

Jesus could have argued with them on their interpretation of Sabbath laws. But He didn't. Instead, He drove home the real issue to make His point.

Jesus intentionally worked on the Sabbath as a sign pointing to who He is.

He is Lord of the Sabbath. Lord of Creation. All that exists was created by His spoken Word, and nothing exists without it. God is always working to uphold and sustain what He has created and Jesus does the same. Jesus is indeed making Himself equal with God.

That's why there's increasing opposition against Him from this point onward. Religious Jews are less upset about what Jesus is doing, and much more upset about who He is saying He is.

Jesus made His point and now He will engage the religious Jews further in this regard.

3. Read John 5:19-20. In the ESV it begins with the word "so" indicating that Jesus' words in the following verses are a direct response based on the contents of verse 18.
    a. With which phrase does Jesus begin His response in verse 19, and what does this indicate? (Hint: Look back at Week 1, Day 3 of your homework.)

    b. In verse 20, Jesus says you will see greater works than these. What work specifically would His hearers have had in mind? What had just happened to make them start questioning Jesus?

---

[1] D.A. Carson, The Gospel According to John, Grand Rapids, Michigan, William B Eerdmans Publishing Company, 1991; page 247.

4. Read John 5:21-25. What two things does Jesus say the Father has given to Him?

And many of those who sleep in the dust of the earth shall awake, some to everlasting life, and some to shame and everlasting contempt. Daniel 12:2

5. Why has the Father given these things to the Son, according to John 5:23?

6. We see Jesus make two more authoritative statements in verses 24 and 25. What point is He making with each statement?

7. Read John 5:26-29. As you do, remember that John is showing us the signs that point to Jesus as the Messiah. Now flip back to Daniel 7:13-14. Here we read a description of the promised Messiah that God shared with Daniel in a vision.
    a. By what name is the Messiah introduced in verse 13?

    b. What is given to Him in verse 14, and how long will He reign?

    c. Knowing that religious Jews would have had extensive knowledge of Old Testament Scriptures, how would they have interpreted Jesus' statement in John 5:27?

Jesus affirms what they suspect. They were angry because He was making Himself equal with God—He gives them Old Testament Scripture to prove it. He tells them that they found it astounding when a man who had been impotent for a life span got up and walked, but they would see more than this—they would see a grave opened and a man walk out. (At this point, I'm itching to race to John 11 or John 20, but we'll wait. If you want to read ahead in John 11 though, don't let me stop you!)

8. Read John 5:30-43.
    a. I'm pretty sure the religious Jews were feeling a little hot under the collar at the thought that this man would have the authority to pass judgment on them. Jesus, who knew their thoughts as He does ours, assures them that His judgment is just. Why? (verse 30)

    b. In this passage, what five things does Jesus say bear witness to Him, or testify regarding Him?
       i. Verse 33:

       ii. Verse 36 (two things):

       iii. Verse 37:

       iv. Verse 39:

    c. In this passage, Jesus says some hard things to His listeners. What are some of the tough truths Jesus puts forth?
       i. Verse 38:

       ii. Verse 40:

       iii. Verse 42:

       iv. Verse 43:

Those are hard words. And if the religious Jews were tempted to disregard them, they had to disregard how Jesus opened this part of His talk, by saying that His judgment is just because it seeks the will of His Father. God. The same God they made all these rules up for. The same God they said they wanted to honor by following His Law.

9. Are there any tough truths of Jesus that you are wrestling with? What is keeping you from accepting His authority in these areas?

Jesus ends this talk with the words that must have been the hardest for them to hear.

10. Read John 5:44-47.
    a. In verse 44, what does Jesus say is at the heart of their unbelief?

    b. Why do you think He described God as the only God?

    c. In verse 45, who does Jesus say they have set their hope on?

    d. Who will therefore pass judgment on them?

In the prologue to his Gospel, John wrote that, from Moses, the Jews had received one kind of grace: the Law. From Jesus they received more grace and more truth. (John 1:16-17) The truth He spoke to them maybe didn't feel like grace in the moment, but He tells them in verse 34 that He says these things so that they might be saved. That is grace. Being willing to speak hard truths if it will save someone.

As we close today, let's lean into the hard words rather than run away from them.

What have you set your hope on? How have these things let you down? Do you see how in failing you, they also accuse you by revealing that they are not a trustworthy place for your hope to be set? Do you see how their failing you is grace if it sends you looking for the One who will not let your hope down?

The signs all point to Him; it begins and ends with the One who was the Word at the beginning. If you will believe in Him, you will pass from death to life. You will not sit under judgment because you will have done the only thing that will earn your salvation: believing in Jesus Christ and coming to Him for life.

That is grace upon grace.

Set your hope fully on the grace that will be brought to you at the revelation of Jesus Christ.
1 Peter 1:13b

Day Three: Do You See the Signs? (John 6:1-14)

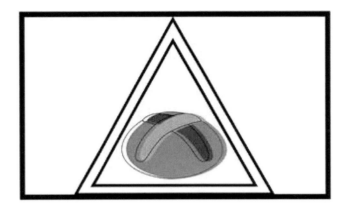

**Blessed art thou, O Lord our God, King of the universe,
who bringest forth bread from the earth.
(Common form of Jewish thanksgiving)**

You usually enter another person's home in the most expected, straight-forward manner possible. Typically, you walk to the front door, ring the doorbell, then wait for someone to open the door and usher you into the room designated for greeting visitors. If that's what you did at my house, most days you'd see very little in the way of clutter. The coat tree would be mostly empty, waiting for our guests to use. The front mat would be clean and tidy, with ample room for our company's shoes. Most days (am I kidding myself, here? Do I just really want it to be most days?) the clutter near the front door is limited or non-existent so that upon entering our house, you would form a certain impression of our family.

I don't imagine many of us would pull up to someone's house, look at the front door, and think, "way too predictable," then look for another way in. Opening gates and climbing fences in search of a back door entrance is definitely frowned upon. But imagine that you tried this.

If you came in my back door, your impression of us would undergo a marked change. In the summertime, you'd see swimsuits and towels bunched in a corner, pool noodles and goggles strewn about, and flip flops and sandals kicked off in carefree abandon. If it was winter, just replace all I described with hockey equipment and snow gear.

You might be wondering if anyone ever cleans at our house. Yes. Thoroughly and frequently. But ours is a busy house with four children and the sheer act of living flies in the face of most cleaning efforts.

Coming in my front door might impress you with the idea that we are tidy, organized, and that everything has a place and is in its place. Coming in the back door will give you a better picture of who we actually are.

Interesting? Maybe. Relevant? How?

Well, today we are coming at our passage of Scripture through the metaphorical back door. Instead of opening the front door and reading John 6:1-14 right off the bat, we'll wander through some bits and pieces of history that will tell us who the people in this story really are. If you're like me, this sounds like fun. (If I wouldn't get arrested for doing so, I'd habitually wander through people's back doors, purely out of curiosity.)

Remember back in week one when the religious Jews were trying to figure out who John the Baptist was? They came at it through the front door. "Who are you?" John the Baptist answered, "I am not the Christ." They followed this up by asking more specifically about two different people.

1. Look back at John 1:19-21. Which two people were the religious leaders asking about?

Moses and Elijah were two heroes from Israel's history. Let's take a quick wander through the rooms of Moses' life. He pops up on the pages of Israel's history at a time when they were enslaved and grossly mistreated. Moses' life is saved by his mother's defiance of Pharaoh's order that all baby boys be killed upon birth. Because of this, Moses ends up being raised in Pharaoh's own palace.

God wasn't blind to His people's suffering or deaf to their cries. He had a plan to save His people and reveal His glory. This plan involved Moses stepping up to take the lead. God appeared to Moses and commanded him to go to Pharaoh and demand the release of the people of Israel.

Pharaoh didn't listen easily. God worked miraculous signs and wonders through Moses before leading His people out of Egypt and through the Red Sea. This path led into a wilderness where God was the only source of provision. He quenched their thirst with water from a rock. He fed their bellies with bread and meat from heaven. For forty years, the people of God wandered through the desert, sheltered by the cloud of God's presence, warmed by His Holy Fire.

2. Read Deuteronomy 8:1-3. What does Moses tell the people of Israel that God was teaching them as He provided for them in the desert?

That is just a bare-bones look at Moses and the period of time when he led God's people. There were many other times in Israel's history when God worked miracles on their behalf. The other extended period of time was during the days of Elijah.

3. Let's turn to the first passage in the Bible where Elijah is mentioned. You'll find it in 1 Kings 17. Read verses 1-6.
   a. What does Elijah prophesy to Ahab in verse 1?

   b. What can you infer will happen in the land because of this?

c. How does God provide for Elijah during his time of hiding?

Isn't it fascinating to read that both Moses and Elijah lived for an extended period of time in utter dependence upon God for their daily bread?

If you were to read the rest of 1 Kings 17, you'd see God use a widow to provide bread for Elijah and then use Elijah to raise this same widow's son from the dead. These are just some of the fascinating stories from Elijah's life. But the next chapter has one of my favourite Elijah stories.

For a long time, God withheld rain and dew from the land because of the wickedness of the people. Finally, God sent Elijah to evil King Ahab with the promise of rain, but it wasn't going to just fall softly from the sky at Elijah's word. There'd be a colossal showdown before the wash-down.

Elijah commanded Ahab to gather all the prophets of Baal on Mount Carmel—the place they believed Baal dwelled. This showdown was going to happen on Baal's home turf and the numbers were stacked in his favour—450 prophets for Baal against Elijah and God.

4. What does Elijah ask the people in 1 Kings 18:21?

Elijah challenges the people to stop hedging their bets and take a stand. But the people stay silent. Elijah puts them and their gods to the test. He commands the prophets of Baal to prepare an altar and a sacrifice, and then to call on Baal to burn up the sacrifice. Baal's priests prepare. They call out. For hours. They limp around the altar. They cut themselves until blood gushes from them. All to silence.

Now it's Elijah's turn to prepare an altar with an offering to God. He sets the altar up with twelve stones, representing the twelve tribes of Israel, then he drenches the altar, the sacrifice, and the ground around it with water. He soaks it with water that would have been precious because of the harshness of the drought. When Elijah is done, he prays, "O LORD, God of Abraham, Isaac, and Israel, let it be known this day that you are God in Israel . . . answer me that this people may know that you, O LORD, are God, and that you have turned their hearts back." (1 Kings 18:36, 37) When Elijah cries out, God comes down. The fire of the LORD falls and consumes not only the offering and the wood, but the stones and the dust as well.

5. According to 1 Kings 18:39, how do the people respond?

Both Moses and Elijah lived uncommon lives and experienced uncommon deaths. In Deuteronomy 34:5-6 we read that God called Moses to the top of a mountain to show Moses the land He was giving to His people, and there, alone on the mountain with God, Moses died. It was the tender hand of God Himself that buried Moses. Just as there was no grave for Moses that the people of Israel could visit, there would be none for the prophet Elijah. 2 Kings 2 tells us that when Elijah's work was done, God came for him with heaven's chariot of fire to carry him, in a whirlwind, to the presence of God.

The life and death of both of these uncommon men pointed to Christ. The religious leaders of Jesus' day had their eyes so fixed on the sign, they missed the One it pointed to.

We've spent some time wandering around some of the back rooms of Israel's history. We've glimpsed some of the clutter they were holding on to. In clinging so tightly to what was precious to them, they entirely missed what it pointed to.

In the passage we looked at yesterday, Jesus told the religious Jews, *you want Moses, okay, but you're not even listening to him. You're not really seeing what he tried to show you. You know your Scriptures so well, but even still you don't see the picture they set before you.*

We're ready to come to our passage today. Before you read it, remember, John did not write his Gospel merely as an account of all the events of Jesus' ministry. He does not write about everything Jesus said or did.

Now Jesus did many other *signs* in the presence of the disciples, which are not written in this book; but *these* are written *so that you may believe that Jesus is the Christ, the Son of God*, and that by believing you may have life in his name. John 20:30-31 (emphasis added)

John is writing his Gospel account to show his readers the same thing Jesus was showing the people during His time on earth. **Come & See** — because really seeing who Jesus is, is literally a life and death matter.

6. Read John 6:1-15.
    a. How might Jesus' act of feeding the 5000 have reminded the Jews of both Moses and Elijah?

    b. What physical need was met?

    c. What spiritual need was exposed?

    d. What evidence is there in this passage that, once again, the people have missed the significance of who Jesus is?

7. Write down John 5:39-40.

It's easy to read these stories and think how foolish the Israelites were. How blind. Yet, spiritual blindness is just as prevalent today. We, too, can miss Jesus completely.

Like the people of Israel, we can fixate on the law and miss grace. We can be so impressed with the signs and wonders that we miss Who they point to. And we can be so focused on our own expectations of who God is and what He should do that we fail to see what He is doing right in front of us.

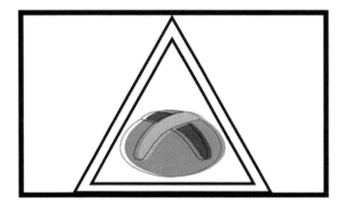

Open our eyes, Lord, that we may see.

Jesus answered them, "Truly, truly, I say to you, you are seeking me, not because you saw signs, but because you ate your fill of the loaves. Do not work for the food that perishes, but for the food that endures to eternal life, which the Son of Man will give you.
John 6:26-27

Day Four: Bread of Life (John 6:16-59)

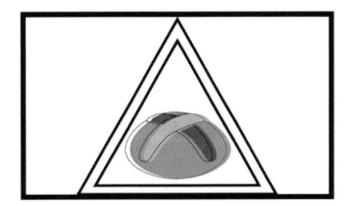

And the Word became flesh and dwelt among us, and we have seen his glory, glory as of the only Son from the Father, full of grace and truth. For from his fullness we have all received, grace upon grace. For the law was given through Moses; grace and truth came through Jesus Christ. No one has ever seen God; the only God, who is at the Father's side, he has made him known. John 1:14, 16-18

Yesterday we did a bit of wandering. Today we come at things directly. Our passage today is lengthy and can be difficult, so we'll break it down, working through it in sections.

1. Read John 6:16-21.
    a. What situation, according to verses 16-18, do the disciples find themselves in?

    b. How does Jesus respond to the situation in verses 19-20?

    c. How do the disciples respond to Jesus in verse 21?

2. Read John 6:22-29. The crowd following Jesus asks a question that seems to be coming at the real issue through the back door. But Jesus answers by busting open the front door. He sees into our hearts and knows our motives.
    a. What does Jesus say they are really after and what are they missing?

    b. How do they respond in verse 28?

    c. What is Jesus' response in verse 29?

d. Is Jesus concerned more with their works or their heart? Explain.

3. Read John 6:30-31. On whom are they once again setting their hope?

4. Read John 6:32-36. What is Jesus' response to their misplaced hope?

Because of the age in which we live, we miss some of the punch of John chapter six. If you could turn the calendar back about 2000 years and be a part of that crowd, you'd know by the rumble in your belly that food was important and, for the working class (most of society), hard to come by. Most of your time and energy would be spent working for food. And the menu you were working for was pretty short. Bread (wheat if you were wealthier, barley if you were not) and fish were staples in that time and place.

Now imagine a man shows up in your area and feeds a massive crowd of people. What you work hard for day in and day out, year in and year out, what you know you need simply to sustain life, appears from his hands—seemingly effortlessly. Can you see why the people who witnessed the miracle tried to take Jesus by force and make Him king? (John 6:15) A man like this could not only raise up an army, he could feed it!

We've seen this over and over in John's Gospel. Jesus is trying to open the people's eyes to spiritual realities, but they have a hard time getting past the physical.

5. Read John 6:37-58.
    a. Why were the people grumbling against Jesus in verses 41-42?

    b. What does Jesus say, in verses 48-51, is the difference between Moses' bread and His? (Think about what Jesus is revealing over and over again to the people.)

    c. The Hebrew people had a saying: "flesh and blood," meaning the whole person unto death.[2] With this in mind, and all you've learned so far in John's Gospel, what do you think is at the heart of verses 53-58?

---

[2] Kostenberger, Andreas J., John, 2004, Baker Academic Grand Rapids, Michigan, page 216.

I have this thing where I don't like to cook or eat meat that looks like the animal it is. Whole pigs on a spit make my stomach turn. An entire fish lying on a plate makes me feel like I can't escape the gaze of that unseeing eye. I prefer to be more removed from what's actually happening when I eat.

What is actually happening? Well, my burger was once a cow. The bun it's nestled between comes from wheat that was cut down and ground up. My grilled chicken breast was once the pride of some chicken strutting around a barnyard, and the lettuce I rest it on had to be pulled up and harvested so I could enjoy it. What most of us do not see as clearly as Jesus' listeners would have seen is that for us to eat, something has to die. It's us or them. The fish will give its life or the people do not eat and lose theirs. The barley or wheat must be cut down or the people have no bread and will go hungry. That is the physical reality which is true virtually every time we eat. It is a sign of a much deeper spiritual reality.

Life must come through death; it is a necessary substitution.
His life for ours. Or we die. Eternally.[3]

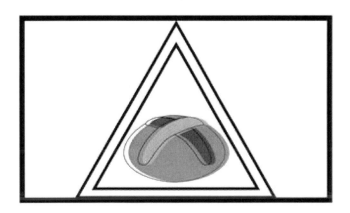

Physical death comes to all. Any measures we take to prolong our physical lives are simply that, a prolonging. Spiritual death is a different matter. There is One who came down as bread from heaven. Whoever feeds on this bread will live forever.

The God who delivered His people from slavery and death is still the way to freedom and life. The One who fed and sustained His people in the wilderness will feed and sustain His people for all of eternity with the splendor of His presence. The same hand that buried Moses and carried Elijah to heaven will carry all who feed on Him to the eternal feast of His presence.

Jesus said to them, "I am the bread of life; whoever comes to me shall not hunger, and whoever believes in me shall never thirst." John 6:35

---

[3] Carson, D. (2001). Part 5: Jesus the Bread of God (John 6:25-71): Portraits of Jesus in John's Gospel. Resources.thegospelcoalition.org accessed September 29, 2017. (Carson D. , 2001)

Day Five: Personal Reflection

Pick one or two of the questions below, and journal, pray, or reflect on them.

1. **John 5:6, 8 When Jesus saw him lying there and knew that he had already been there a long time, he said to him, "Do you want to be healed?" Jesus said to him, "Get up, take up your bed, and walk."**

   John 1:1, 4 In the beginning was the Word, and the Word was with God, and the Word was God. In him was life, and the life was the light of men.

   Jesus' acts of physical healing were signs pointing to something greater—spiritual healing and eternal life in Him. This gift of life is for everyone, yet like the man at the pool in Bethesda, we often look past the Giver and see only the gift. Has your response to Jesus' gift of eternal life looked more like the lame man who was healed at the pool, or more like the Samaritan woman at the well? Have you, like the lame man, looked past the Giver and been content with the gift, thinking it was enough? How can you seek more of Christ this week?

2. **Deuteronomy 8:2-3 And you shall remember the whole way that the LORD your God has led you these forty years in the wilderness, that he might humble you, testing you to know what was in your heart, whether you would keep his commandments or not. And he humbled you and let you hunger and fed you with manna, which you did not know, nor did your fathers know, that he might make you know that man does not live by bread alone, but man lives by every word that comes from the mouth of the LORD.**

   During their forty years in the wilderness, God taught the Israelites that their only hope of life, their only source of survival, was complete and utter dependence on Him. This is true for all of us. How has God taught you the same lesson? In what ways did He humble you and let you hunger, only to feed you with the Bread of Life? How are you intentionally depending upon God each day for your daily bread?

3. **John 5:39-40, 45 You search the Scriptures because you think that in them you have eternal life; and it is they that bear witness about me, yet you refuse to come to me that you may have life. Do not think that I will accuse you to the Father. There is one who accuses you: Moses, on whom you have set your hope.**

   Like the people of Israel, we can fixate on the law and miss grace. We can be so impressed with signs and wonders that we miss Who they point to. And we can be so focused on our own expectations of who God is and what He should do that we fail to see what He is doing right in front of us. What expectations do you have of God—how He should act and what He should do? How might these expectations blind your eyes to the works God is doing right in front of you each day? Like the Israelites, have you set your hope on a "sign" that points to Christ instead of on Christ, Himself? Are you willing to let go of all you're holding onto and cling to Christ alone?

Teaching Session Four: These are Hard Teachings
(John 6:60 - 7:52)

❖ Basic biology: if you are alive, you will face hunger and thirst every day. Our survival depends on finding that which will fill our hunger and quench our thirst.

❖ Just like there is no physical life without food and water, there is no spiritual life apart from Jesus Christ the Creator, who spoke all things into being, and without whom nothing would exist.

This is a hard saying; who can listen to it? John 6:60

❖ The teachings are hard. Many don't like what they hear, and they turn away.

Simon Peter answered him, "Lord, to whom shall we go? You have the words of eternal life, and we have believed, and have come to know, that you are the Holy One of God." John 6:68-69

❖ If, like Peter declared, Jesus is the Holy One of God, where else could we turn for life?

There is salvation in no one else, for there is no other name under heaven given among men by which we must be saved. Acts 4:12

❖ **Feast of Passover or Unleavened Bread:** commemorates Israel's deliverance from Egypt and hints at salvation through the blood of the lamb.

❖ **Feast of Weeks or Pentecost:** celebrated 50 days after the Passover when God revealed His Law to Moses and the people. The 50 days between Passover and the Feast of Weeks, or Pentecost, are the days of Counting the Omar.
  ◆ Do you think it is coincidence that every post-resurrection appearance of Jesus occurred on the days of Counting the Omar?

The law was given through Moses but grace and truth came through Jesus Christ! John 1:17

❖ **Feast of Tabernacles:** The word "tabernacle" simply means tent. For eight days, the Jewish people erected tents, or booths—hastily erected temporary dwellings—and lived in them to remember how God, after freeing them from slavery, provided for and protected them every day for 40 years.
  ◆ The wilderness did not have the necessary elements for survival. It was a desert—there was no stable and reliable sources of food or water. The heat of the desert sun was too intense during the day, and the absence of it in the night made the cold darkness too severe. But for every day that this continued, they had the visible presence of God. They were never alone. (Exodus 40:38)
  ◆ Water quenched their thirst and grew their daily bread. That's why, throughout the Old Testament, water is a symbol for life.

Jesus stood up and cried out, "If anyone thirsts, let him come to me and drink. Whoever believes in me, as the Scripture has said, 'Out of his heart will flow rivers of living water.'" John 7:37-38

"You search the Scriptures because you think that in them you have eternal life; and it is they that bear witness about me, yet you refuse to come to me that you may have life." John 5:39-40

❖ Come to me, says Jesus, the source of living water you can buy without price.

❖ God created every single person who will ever live to feel hunger and thirst every day of their existence. You will never escape your hunger and your thirst. Where will you go to satisfy them?

❖ All who hunger and thirst can come to Jesus in faith, knowing that He will keep them until the day of the great ingathering.

Session Notes:

WEEK FOUR: COME & SEE!

We saw in our most recent teaching session that the Feast of Tabernacles had elaborate daily ceremonies of water and light. Jesus reoriented these rituals as signs which pointed to Him.

This week we'll see that, as Jesus nears the cross, He speaks with more urgency and clarity. He clearly states that He is the Christ, the One they've been waiting for. But the clearer His message, the more opposition it attracts. Jesus knows His public ministry is winding to a close so He implores His listeners to open their eyes and see that He is the One their Scriptures point to and that every promise will be fulfilled in Him

As you begin your homework this week, open by reading the passage from Isaiah 42, written below. When you finish your homework at the end of the week, come back to this passage and meditate on how Jesus fulfilled it.

The LORD'S Chosen Servant

Thus says God, the LORD, who created the heavens and stretched them out, who spread out the earth and what comes from it, who gives breath to the people on it and spirit to those who walk in it:
"I am the LORD; I have called you in righteousness; I will take you by the hand and keep you; I will give you as a covenant for the people, a light for the nations, to open the eyes that are blind, to bring out the prisoners from the dungeon, from the prison those who sit in darkness.
Isaiah 42:5-7

In him was life, and the life was the light of men.
The light shines in the darkness, and the darkness has not overcome it.
John 1:4-5

Day One: The Light of the World (John 8:12)

Can life exist without light?

Light can be defined somewhat differently, depending on how you attempt to understand it. The scientific definition of light is complex and beyond my understanding. But I don't have to be a scientist to see that light makes things visible. It illuminates and provides understanding. Light is tightly connected to life. Scripture teaches us this same concept.

In him was life, and the life was the light of men. John 1:4

Our last teaching session opened our eyes to the practice and symbolism of the Feast of Tabernacles, the yearly festival during which Jews remembered their desert wanderings. We saw how John, a Jew writing to Jews, intentionally ordered his Gospel to point to Jesus as the fulfillment of the wilderness wanderings: Jesus was the Bread from heaven, the Water from the rock, and their Light in the darkness. Today we look more closely at Jesus as the Light.

Instead of starting in John's Gospel, however, we're going all the way back to the beginning.

1. Start by reading Genesis 1:1-4.
    a. How was the earth described before God spoke?

    b. What was the first phrase God spoke in His Word? (Note: this is also His first act of creation.)

    c. Skip ahead to Genesis 1:14-15. What was the purpose of the lights God created?

2. Turn to Exodus 13:21-22. The Israelites have just fled Egypt at God's command. They enter the desert in the middle of the night, under the cover of darkness. But the darkness would not remain.

   a. Why did the LORD go before the people of Israel?

   b. How did He go before the people of Israel?

   c. How often did the LORD go before the people of Israel?

Into the dark void, God spoke and there was light. God separated the light from the darkness and put lights in the heavens to be signs, marking off time. There was light and day, but night still came and darkness prevailed for a set period of time.

God's people waited in the darkness of slavery until the time was right. When it was, God came down to deliver them with mighty and marvelous signs. He set His people free and led them out of Egypt towards their Promised Land. But God did not deliver His people and then depart. On the entire journey from bondage to freedom, God was their constant and visible light. Every day of their wanderings, God's people walked in the light of His presence.

How precious is your steadfast love, O God!
The children of mankind take refuge in the shadow of your wings. They feast on the
abundance of your house, and you give them drink from the river of your delights.
For with you is the fountain of life; in your light do we see light. Psalm 36:7-9

Through the heat of the day when the sun's power could have harmed them, God sheltered His people with the cloud of His presence. When night crept in and the darkness could have overwhelmed them, God's fire held it at bay. In a barren land where hunger and thirst could have overcome them, God sustained them with bread from heaven and water from a rock. The light that illuminated every part of the journey was the truth that life came from God.

But over time, God's people forgot how His presence sustained them. They walked away from the light of God's path and onto their own. The darkness disoriented them. They lost their sure footing. They couldn't find peace, justice, or truth, and salvation was far from them. All because they turned their backs on God. (Isaiah 59) They needed a beacon of hope, a light that would illuminate their way back to the Father. But there was no one to intervene in their desperate situation.

So God intervened. He promised to come to their rescue and be their deliverer. "A Redeemer will come to Zion for those who will turn from their sin," says the LORD. (Isaiah 59:20)

3. Read Isaiah 60:1-3.
    a. What is the title of this section?

    b. How does God announce the coming Redeemer in verse 1?

    c. Who will benefit from this coming Redeemer, according to verse 3?

    d. Skip ahead a little bit and pick up the account in verses 18-22 with a continued description of what God has said is coming. What created elements are replaced in verses 19 and 20, and what are they replaced by?

I have come into the world as light, so that whoever believes in me may not remain in darkness. John 12:46

Knowing their Scriptures, the faithful among the people of Israel waited for the time Isaiah had spoken of. Though exiled, some still waited and watched. When they returned, some did so with eyes and ears open. They posted a guard while they laboured to rebuild their temple, and some also set a watchman over their hearts. (You can read about this in the book of Nehemiah if you're interested.)

Then one day, while a priest whose ears and eyes were open was on duty in the temple, a messenger from God appeared. The wait was over.

4. Turn to Luke 1:68-69. Upon receiving the news that, not only would he have a son, but this son would prepare the way for God's coming, what three things does John the Baptist's father bless God for?

5. At the end of his prophecy in Luke 1:78-79, how does Zechariah refer to the Messiah, and what does he say He will do?

6. Matthew's Gospel begins with a genealogy and a birth announcement. There is a brief account of Jesus' childhood, baptism, and temptation. But when Matthew is ready to begin telling of the good news of Jesus, how does he choose to begin in Matthew 4:16?

"Awake, O sleeper, and arise from the dead, and Christ will shine on you." Ephesians 5:14

7. Write down Jesus' words in John 8:12.

The bread, the water, the light — all point to Him.

When the Jews of Jesus' day celebrated the Feast of Tabernacles, every evening, except for on the intervening Sabbath, four young priests would enter the Court of the Women. This area was not designated especially for Jewish women, it was the place beyond which Jewish women could not pass and it lay just beyond the Court of the Gentiles, on the other side of the Beautiful Gate. In this court there were four massive, golden candlesticks—approximately 75 feet tall— with golden bowls on the top of them. The four young men would climb ladders and fill these bowls with oil. Taking wicks made from worn out priestly undergarments, they lit the candles. Because the temple sat on a hill above the rest of the city, the glow from these massive candlesticks would have illuminated every courtyard in Jerusalem. And every night, after the great golden candles were lit, God's people would celebrate under their light. The Levitical orchestra played while the people danced and sang praises all through the night, celebrating light in defiance of darkness.

In this context, Jesus declared, "**I am the Light of the World**." The true light had come.

He has delivered us from the domain of darkness and transferred us to the kingdom of his beloved Son, in whom we have redemption, the forgiveness of sins. Colossians 1:13

The Kingdom of Light has come—it's now among us. But the battle still rages. Even though it's defeated, the kingdom of darkness hasn't given up its fight. The victory is won, but the war isn't over. Yet.

8. Turn to the final chapters of the final book of the Bible and read Revelation 21:22-25. What description does John give of the New Jerusalem?

If the victory cry sends out a hollow echo in your life right now, know that though the darkness of battle might dim some of the light now, one day, darkness will be defeated. Forever. This prophecy is yet unfulfilled, but its fulfillment is as sure as all the prophecies Jesus fulfilled when He walked the earth more than 2000 years ago. You can bet your life on it.

9. In John 8:12, what three words does Jesus speak after saying that He is the light of the world?

Do you see the consequence Jesus relates to His announcement?
The Light has come – will we follow?

From the day we heard, we have not ceased to pray for you, asking that you may be filled with the knowledge of his will in all spiritual wisdom and understanding, so as to walk in a manner worthy of the Lord, fully pleasing to him, bearing fruit in every good work and increasing in the knowledge of God. May you be strengthened with all power, according to his glorious might, for all endurance and patience with joy, giving thanks to the Father, who has qualified you to share in the inheritance of the saints in light. He has delivered us from the domain of darkness and transferred us to the kingdom of his beloved Son, in whom we have redemption, the forgiveness of sins. Colossians 1:9-13

Day Two: I Am He (John 8:12-30)

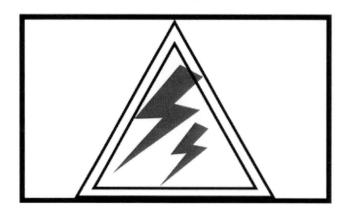

Have you ever been listening to the radio, or watching TV, when a warning interrupted regularly scheduled programming?
How did you react? What factors influenced your reaction?

The advanced technological age we live in has profoundly impacted many aspects of day-to-day life. The field of meteorology might not be the first to pop into your mind, but it's an area that has seen significant improvement with increasing technology. Scientists can now predict dangerous weather far sooner than they could in the past, allowing them to put better early warning systems in place.

The psychology surrounding early warning systems is interesting. I would have thought that being able to increase the time between the warning and the danger was a good thing. I assumed people would want as much notice as possible, and that upon receiving it, they would act quickly and decisively. Oddly, this tends not to be the case.

Researchers have found that when given too much advance warning, people become complacent. They get tired of waiting for the promised danger to arrive and quickly go back to normal. In many cases, people need to see the danger approaching with their own eyes before they feel compelled to take action.[4] (Mitchell, 2017)

Why would people not respond to warnings? Mike Smith, Senior Vice President of AccuWeather Enterprise Solutions and author of Warnings: The True Story of How Science Tamed the Weather, gives several reasons for this strange behaviour. He says that people are often too lazy or too busy. And then there's social pressure. People worry that seeking shelter under clear skies makes them look wimpy. They'd rather take their chances with the danger

---

[4] Chaffin Mitchell; Psychology of warnings: Why do people ignore important weather alerts?, February 7, 2017, AccuWeather: https://www.accuweather.com/en/weather-news/psychology-of-warnings-why-do-people-ignore-weather-alerts/70000135

and be seen as fearless and courageous. Smith writes that people need to hear warnings from someone they trust or from more than one source in order for them to take warnings seriously.[5]

The same is true of spiritual warnings. We read about complacency in the face of approaching danger over and over again in Scripture. People who receive warnings ignore the message, and end up suffering the consequences of their apathy.

In our passage today, Jesus warns His listeners that He is the only way to salvation. But rather than hear the warning, His listeners are distracted by the Messenger. They don't believe the warning because they don't believe the One who gives it. So, instead of life, sadly, they choose death.

1. Turn to our passage for today and read John 8:12-30.
   a. What does Jesus say is true about Himself, and what does He say is true about His listeners in verse 14?

   b. What question do Jesus' listeners ask in verse 19, and how does Jesus respond?

   c. What warning does Jesus give His listeners in verse 24?

   d. What question do His listeners ask in verse 25, and how does Jesus answer?

   e. What does Jesus tell His listeners that they will know, and how/when will they come to this knowledge? (verse 28)

Jesus' listeners wanted to know who Jesus was, who His Father was, where He came from, and where He was going. While we might struggle to see it, Jesus gives them a clear answer. The answer is in His repeated phrase of identification, "I am he."

Jesus uses a phrase that appears numerous times on the lips of the Jewish prophet whose name meant, "Yahweh is salvation." Let's turn to the book of Isaiah to see this for ourselves.

2. For each of the following references, record the claim behind every "I am he" statement.
   a. Isaiah 41:4

   b. Isaiah 43:10-13, 25

   c. Isaiah 46:3-4

---

[5] Ibid.

d. Isaiah 48:12

The answer to who Jesus is, is the hinge of history. It is the most important question that each of us must answer. It is the trial whose verdict will determine sentencing for all eternity.

As His time on earth grows short, Jesus sounds the warning loud and clear. *You want to know who I am and I am giving you the answer. What will you do with it? Step out of the darkness and into the light! Follow Me, the One who says to you, I am the Light!* Will you hear Jesus' words that He is the Christ, and believe He is who He says He is, or will you ignore the warning and die in your sins? I know that sounds harsh, but friends, when the danger is real and terrible, the warning should be clear.

Jesus holds up the definitive piece of evidence in this trial: the cross.

3. In John 8:22, how do Jesus' listeners attempt to understand Jesus' words that they cannot go where He will go?

They are close to the truth; Jesus will die. But He will die at their hands, not His own. Yet they are also close to the truth in that He will choose death. He will choose to lay down His life. They will not take it from Him against His will.

The cross is the turning point of history in that it reveals most clearly who Jesus is. Only a Saviour who is also God can, through dying, defeat death and emerge from its bonds with the victorious shout of eternal life.

We are recipients of the best early warning system of all time. Wouldn't it seem foolish to grow tired while waiting for danger to arrive, so stop watching for it and get on with our lives? Wouldn't it seem risky to want to see death and destruction with our own eyes before running from it, only to find out it was too late? And wouldn't you rather have people think you were foolish for seeking safety and taking shelter before the danger was visible, instead of getting caught up in the danger of thinking you'd at least kept your dignity intact?

Let's run to the Light and see this as true courage rather than lack of it.

There is salvation in no one else! God has given no other name under heaven by which we must be saved. Acts 4:12 NLT

Day Three: The Truth Will Set You Free (John 8:31-59)

In our study yesterday, we saw Jesus being clear with His listeners about who He was. The passage we studied ended with John 8:30: "As He was saying these things, many believed in Him." The result of Jesus' words was that many believed.

But Jesus wasn't done teaching yet, because those who turned to Him in faith, were still in the darkness of misunderstanding. They still did not see their need for a Savior, so the Light of the World shone His light of truth on their confusion and unbelief. *I AM, and there is no other.*

So Jesus said to the Jews who had believed him, "If you abide in my word, you are truly my disciples, and you will know the truth, and the truth will set you free." John 8:31-32

1. In the verse above, what word connects what Jesus is now saying with what He said before?

2. Who is Jesus speaking to?

3. What does Jesus say the result of abiding will be?

Some who had heard, believed. But this doesn't cause Jesus to respond by celebrating His popularity, or proclaiming His fame. Instead, He challenges those who say they believe in Him. Will they abide? Will they remain? Will they hold on?

4. Turn to the passage in your Bible and read John 8:31-33. What thought do these new believers latch on to? (verse 33)

If you are familiar with Israel's history, you might wonder at their statement. Exodus tells of how God's chosen people were enslaved in Egypt. The Kings, the Chronicles, the Prophets — they all tell of how Babylon and Assyria, the Medes and the Persians, captured, exiled, and subjugated the people of Israel. And the daily reality of the people talking to Jesus was that they lived as a conquered nation under the power of Rome. So what were they talking about?

5. Turn to Leviticus 25:39-42. What Law regarding slavery and the people of Israel did God set forth?

The Jews believed that freedom was their birthright no matter how poor they were. They knew that in a physical sense, they'd been captives in the past. But in a spiritual sense, they still saw themselves as free because they believed that even in captivity, they were under God's authority not under the authority of the nations over them. (For an example of what led them to this thinking, read Deuteronomy 28:25-68)

They interpreted their physical reality in light of what they believed was their spiritual reality. And they were on the right path with this line of thinking, they just weren't far enough along it. God was in authority over them. He directed their paths, and only in Him was true freedom. But their eyes were pointed down on the letter of the law, so they missed the One God placed in the middle of their path—the One the Law was pointing them to. If they wouldn't live in the freedom God was providing for them, were they really free?

6. How does Jesus shine the light of truth on their situation in John 8:34?

Doesn't this remind you of the time Jesus challenged Nicodemus' assumptions of privilege in John chapter 3? The Jews believed that because they were physically in the family of Abraham they were promised eternal life. They believed because they were spiritually in the family of God, they were free. Jesus challenged these assumptions.

The next passage refers to a father-son relationship which in that time and culture was more of a reference to shared characteristics, attitudes, and behaviour, and less a reference to shared DNA.

7. Read John 8:34-59. What evidence do you see that Jesus is making this point in these verses?

8. Which two fathers does Jesus contrast in verses 42-44, and what character traits does He attribute to each?

9. Look more closely at verses 39-41 before turning to read Genesis 15:6 and 22:16-18. Based on these verses, what works of Abraham do you think Jesus is referring to in John 8:39-41?

10. What two questions does Jesus ask His listeners in verse 46?

Our legal system places the burden of proof upon the prosecution. It's the job of whoever is making the accusation of guilt to produce valid and reliable evidence to justify the charge. In criminal law, because the consequences are more severe, and include loss of freedom and possibly even loss of life in some jurisdictions, the burden of proof is greater and must be made beyond a reasonable doubt. Civil law carries a lighter burden of conviction and so the burden of proof is also less. Yet, it must still be clear, convincing, and outweigh the evidence presented against.

Jesus places the burden of proof upon His accusers. They don't accuse Him in His conduct because they can't.

Jesus' second question, however, poses a serious dilemma to those who listen: What if He is telling the truth about who He is?

If there was any ambiguity left on the part of His listeners, Jesus doesn't allow it to remain.

11. In John 8:56, whose day does Jesus say Abraham rejoiced to see?

Before the mountains were brought forth, or ever you had formed the earth and the world, from everlasting to everlasting you are God. Psalm 90:2

12. What are the last words Jesus spoke in John chapter 8?

Remember who Moses was to them? He was their guy, their hero. He was the one who asked God, *when your people ask who sent me, what should I say to them? Who shall I say is behind this; what name should I give them?* He was the one God answered by saying, "I AM WHO I AM. Say this to the people of Israel, I AM has sent me to you. This is my name forever, and thus I am to be remembered throughout all generations." (Exodus 3:14-15)

If even one of Jesus' listeners hung onto the idea that they were reading too much into His words, or thought maybe they were jumping to rash conclusions, Jesus erased their doubt. With absolute authority He declared that He was God.

His accusers couldn't present a burden of proof strong enough to convict Him. Yes, they had the fact that Jesus healed on the Sabbath, but if Jesus was who He said He was, He couldn't be charged or convicted for the very thing it was His job to do. Oh, how they want to charge, convict, and declare Him guilty! They longed to hand out the sentence attached to blasphemy: death.

The people didn't believe His claim so, in profound irony, they turned their backs on Him and plotted His death.

How was this the height of irony? The Jews had this conversation with Jesus during the Feast of Tabernacles. Each day of the feast, priests would perform a daily ritual during which the people would reflect on how their forefathers turned their backs on God to worship the sun, vowing that they would never do the same. They vowed to keep their eyes on the Lord, their faces pointed towards Him. But when God came to them in the person of His Son, they, too, turned their backs on Him.

Freedom, truth, life, and light are all wrapped up in the person of Jesus Christ. The Son, who came to make the Father known.

I am sending you to them to open their eyes and turn them from darkness to light, and from the power of Satan to God, so that they may receive forgiveness of sins and a place among those who are sanctified by faith in me. Acts 26:17b-18

Day Four: The Blind Will See (John 9)

Today's passage is a wonderful story. In sharp phrases and quick-moving scenes, John reveals a fascinating character and a heated confrontation.

Open your Bible to John 9 and read through the account of Jesus healing a man born blind before coming back to answer the following questions.

1. Remembering what we studied yesterday, what was the one action that Jesus could have been charged for if He was not who He said He was? On what day does He heal the blind man?

2. What is the purpose of this encounter between Jesus and the blind man? (verse 3)

3. Read John 1:18.
   a. What work is Jesus doing while He is in the world?

   b. What does Jesus say in John 9:5?

   c. How do you think Jesus' purpose in John 1:18 relates to Him being the Light of the world?

4. In verse 7, how does the blind man respond to Jesus' instructions, and what is the result?

5. Why would the blind man have known who healed him, but not been able to identify Him?

6. What do the Pharisees say in verse 16 in response to the blind man's story?

7. What keeps the blind man's parents from opening their eyes to see the truth?

8. I love the character of the blind man — he seems a little cheeky, but so likeable and honest in his pursuit of the truth. What question does he ask the Pharisees in verse 27, and how is it answered?

9. The blind man becomes increasingly bold as the questions continue. In verse 31, what does he say they (the Jewish people) all know? Based on the miracle Jesus had just performed, what should they all be able to infer about Jesus? (verse 33)

10. Read John 1:9-11 and John 3:19-21. Using these verses to help you, what do think is behind the response in verse 34?

For the Son of Man came to seek and to save the lost. Luke 19:10

11. In verse 35, we see that Jesus intentionally seeks out the blind man. Why?

12. Remembering Jesus' bold claim from John 8:58 yesterday, what is Jesus really asking the man who had been blind in John 9:35?

13. What do verses 35-38 reveal about the man who'd been blind?

14. Are Jesus and the blind man alone when Jesus makes the statement about being the Son of Man? What evidence shows your answer is correct?

15. What do you think Jesus means by His statement in verse 39?

Do you see a man who is wise in his own eyes? There is more hope for a fool than for him. Proverbs 26:12

At the conclusion of John 8, Jesus made the definitive statement that He was God; the I AM. When the Jews tried to stone Him for blasphemy, Jesus left the temple. The Glory of God in the flesh departed from the very place the Jews most expected to see God's glory, and the place they most longed to see it. They were as blind to its presence as they were to its departure.

Jesus left the temple and saw a man born without physical sight. Because His purpose for coming to earth was to reveal God to the world, Jesus kneaded dirt and spittle together. He could have just spoken a word. Instead, in violation of the Sabbath law, Jesus kneaded.

The One sent from the Father instructed the blind man to go to the pool of Siloam, the same pool the priests would go to get water for the Feast of Tabernacle ceremonies, and wash his eyes. When the man obeyed the source of Living Water, his darkness was washed away and he saw. The Light of the World opened eyes that had only seen darkness and the man who was no longer blind, worshipped.

Hear, you deaf, and look, you blind, that you may see! Isaiah 42:18

Those who thought they knew, who were sure they saw, scorned the blind man and walked away from the Light of Truth into darkness. The very presence of the Light and the Truth brought judgment. In John 8:31, Jesus told His listeners that those who remained in His word would know the truth and be free. In John 9:41, He tells His listeners that they would remain in their sin because they chose not to see.

Jesus was put on trial for His actions towards the blind man, but at the end of the story, it's His listeners who are judged. The Light had come so all could see, but would they choose to?

For God so loved the world, that he gave his only Son, that whoever believes in him should not perish but have eternal life. For God did not send his Son into the world to condemn the world, but in order that the world might be saved through him. Whoever believes in him is not condemned, but whoever does not believe is condemned already, because he has not believed in the name of the only Son of God.
Whoever believes in the Son has eternal life; whoever does not obey the Son shall not see life, but the wrath of God remains on him. John 3:16-18, 36

Day Five: Personal Reflection

Pick one or two of the questions below, and journal, pray, or reflect on them.

1. **John 8:12 I am the light of the world. Whoever follows me will not walk in darkness, but will have the light of life.**

   Considering Jesus' bold statement that He is the fulfillment of Old Testament prophesy concerning the light to come, the Everlasting light, the light to overcome and swallow the darkness, are you filled with hope or trepidation? How has Jesus been light in your life? How has He illuminated your understanding during this study? How has He uncovered/exposed hidden things? How is Jesus leading you in the light of life?

2. **John 8:31, 32, 34 If you abide in my word, you are truly my disciples, and you will know the truth, and the truth will set you free. Truly, truly, I say to you, everyone who practices sin is a slave to sin.**

   How do you abide in the Word? How has this truth set you free, personally? What would you say to someone who felt ensnared by sin? Have you said it to yourself?

3. **John 9:25 One thing I do know, that though I was blind, now I see.**

   In chapter 9, Jesus demonstrated a sign of healing. This physical healing of blindness pointed to a spiritual reality—having the eyes of your heart opened to who Jesus is. The Pharisees missed the point of the sign and accused Jesus of not being from God because He healed on the Sabbath. This just proved their spiritual blindness. Looking at verses John 9:38-39, how does Jesus open your eyes? How do you let Him keep them open? How does Jesus want you to respond?

Teaching Session Five: Scripture Cannot Be Broken
(John 10:1-42)

❖ Review: John 9
   ◆ Using physical realities to teach spiritual ones, Jesus shone light on the spiritual blindness we are all born into.
   ◆ Jesus issues a warning: some would walk into the light and some would walk away from it.
   ◆ Jewish religious leaders question Jesus about the warning. Was it for them? Was He calling them blind?

❖ John 10 is Jesus' response. How do sheep and shepherds connect to spiritual blindness?

He will tend his flock like a shepherd; he will gather the lambs in his arms; he will carry them in his bosom, and gently lead those that are with young. Isaiah 40:11

❖ God's people saw themselves as God's sheep. That's why God comforted them with the image of Him as their Shepherd. That's also why He warned them with it. (Ezekiel 34)

I am the good shepherd. The good shepherd lays down his life for the sheep. John 10:11

❖ Jesus knows His sheep, and there isn't one thing He wouldn't do for them.

❖ He is the ultimate Shepherd and will deal with the ultimate danger—spiritual death—by laying His life down for the sheep.

❖ Jesus is the Good Shepherd, and Jesus is the door—or as some translations say, the gate—to the sheepfold. Anyone who enters through Jesus will be saved.

How awesome is this place! This is none other than the house of God, and this is the gate of heaven. Genesis 28:17

Open to me the gates of righteousness, that I may enter through them and give thanks to the LORD. This is the gate of the LORD; the righteous shall enter through it. Psalm 118:19-20

View this teaching session at www.unshakenministries.com

❖ Jesus freely admits that He will die. But not because the Jewish religious and political leaders have the authority to take His life. He will die because He chooses to lay it down.

❖ John picks up the story a few months later at the Feast of Dedication (John 10:22-39). It commemorated the rededication of the temple after it'd been desecrated by Antiochus Epiphanes IV in 167 BC. It's the feast we now know as Hanukkah.

Scripture cannot be broken. John 10:35b

❖ Jesus tells them, if you're not going to believe my words, that's one thing. But are you going to deny what your eyes see? Then you really are blind.

❖ We've heard the voice of the Good Shepherd. We've seen. We can't now be called blind without guilt.

❖ Jesus made Himself the gate of salvation and all are invited to come into the fold of God through Him.

God's firm foundation stands, bearing this seal: "The Lord knows those who are his." 2 Timothy 2:19

❖ Our hope that He will one day return for His sheep, is secure.

These are the ones coming out of the great tribulation. They have washed their robes and made them white in the blood of the Lamb.
"Therefore they are before the throne of God, and serve him day and night in his temple; and he who sits on the throne will shelter them with his presence.
They shall hunger no more, neither thirst anymore; the sun shall not strike them, nor any scorching heat.
For the Lamb in the midst of the throne will be their shepherd, and he will guide them to springs of living water, and God will wipe away every tear from their eyes." Revelation 7:14-17

❖ None who respond to the call of the Good Shepherd will be lost.

Session Notes:

_____

_____

_____

_____

_____

_____

_____

_____

_____

_____

_____

_____

_____

_____

_____

_____

_____

_____

_____

_____

_____

_____

_____

_____

_____

WEEK FIVE: COUNTDOWN TO THE SHOWDOWN

The deeper we go into John's Gospel, the more the tension builds. Our passage of study this week is John 11 & 12 and this is where the tension climaxes. Jesus has turned water into wine, He's healed a Roman officer's son from a distance, and He has healed a man who spent what could have been a lifetime as an invalid. Jesus revealed Himself to His disciples when He walked on the water, to the masses when He fed the five thousand, and to religious authorities in particular when He gave sight to a man born blind.

Jesus declared Himself to be the access to heaven, the New Temple, the source of new birth, and the way to eternal life. He pointed to Himself as the Living Water, Bread of Life, and Light of the World. He proclaimed Himself equal with God in creation, judge of all the earth, the fulfillment of Scripture, and the embodiment of truth.

And, most scandalous of all, He claimed to be the I AM: God.

Now Jesus gives the ultimate sign. As decisive proof that He is who He has said, Jesus brings a dead man to life. It's the sign that can't be ignored. The sign that accelerates the countdown to the final showdown.

> **The true light, which gives light to everyone, was coming into the world. He was in the world, and the world was made through him, yet the world did not know him. He came to his own, and his own people did not receive him.**
> **John 1:9-11**

Day One: I AM the Resurrection and the Life (John 11:1-44)

One of the reasons I love John's Gospel is because John is simply an excellent writer. He has the ability to make a story come alive with brilliant phrases that reveal character, and a sense of timing that builds intrigue.

The story we arrive at today is pivotal. It's the climactic and final sign which declares with authority the identity of Jesus, and it's the turning point which marks the end of Jesus' public ministry to the Jews. Once complete, Jesus knows He will have provided them with clear signs. Some will see the signs and the One they point to, and will believe and follow. Others will close their eyes to light and life, ultimately snuffing out both.

Today's story foreshadows the greatest sign of all, which is yet to come.

Begin by reading the story through from start to finish. Enjoy the people who come alive: two sisters who seem like opposites, dramatic Thomas who speaks better than he knows, and the crowds who show up to mourn yet end up witnessing far more than they could have imagined. Savour the story, but most of all, savour the main character: Jesus. Read the story and see Him.

1. Read John 11:1-44 in the ESV.
    a. How is the relationship between Jesus and Lazarus, Martha, and Mary described throughout this passage? (verses 3, 5, 36)

    b. What is the purpose of Lazarus' illness? (verse 4)

    c. Why doesn't Jesus hurry off to Bethany when He gets news that Lazarus is sick? See John 7:6, 8 to help with your answer.

    d. Why are the disciples hesitant to go to Bethany when Jesus says it is time to go? (verse 8)

e. How long has Lazarus been dead by the time Jesus arrives? (verse 17)

Friends of Jesus reach out to Him when their brother falls ill, but rather than respond with immediacy, Jesus stays put. We, the readers, are aware that Jesus knows His friend has died, yet He still insists, not yet. Finally, after His friend has been dead four days, Jesus determines the time is right for Him to arrive on the scene.

This is a familiar theme throughout John. Over and over the author tells us, "His time had not yet come." At the end of chapter 10, we see it again. Though the Jews sought to kill Jesus, He escaped their intentions because the time wasn't right. God was in control. His timing would prevail. But here in chapter 11, the disciples forget this. They know Jesus is a hunted man. That's why He stayed out of Judea. So, you can understand why, when the hunted man tells His friends it's time to go back to the place death chases Him (and by association, them), they question the wisdom of His timing. Wouldn't it be better to wait longer? To give the hunters more time to simmer down, perhaps even to forget? I mean, Lazarus is already dead so it's not like there's a hurry, right?

Jesus gives them a lesson in timing. He reminds them that in the physical realm, they know better than to waste daylight hours with laziness. Dark nights make work difficult and dangerous so they need to take full advantage of the light. As long as the light is shining, they should be doing their necessary work.

But when the fullness of time had come, God sent forth his Son, born of woman, born under the law, to redeem those who were under the law, so that we might receive adoption as sons. Galatians 4:4-5

For while we were still weak, at the right time Christ died for the ungodly. Romans 5:6

2. What is Jesus called in John 11:8 and 11:28?

3. What title does Jesus use to refer to Himself in Matthew 26:18 and John 13:13?

   a. How does He affirm the use of this title in John 13:13?

   b. In Matthew 26:18 what does the Teacher say about His time?

Jesus knew He didn't have much time left. His appointed time was approaching and there was still a lot His followers needed to learn. Jesus wasn't done teaching, and His next lesson would be a game changer. If those who opposed Him wanted to kill Him for claiming to be God, their anger would burn white hot when He showed He was God. So instead of racing to Bethany at the first word of Lazarus' illness, Jesus waited.

4. What lesson did Jesus have in store for those who followed Him when He raised Lazarus from the dead? (verse 15)

5. As students of the Gospel of John, it's time for us to do a little bit of review. What critical lesson was taught in each of the following references?
   a. John 3:3

   b. John 3:14-16

   c. John 4:10, 13

   d. John 5:39-40

   e. John 6:48-51

   f. John 8:12

Jesus lived with singular focus: to show God to the world and to show the world that He was God. He lived to fulfill what Scripture foretold. He stood among His people and proclaimed that their Messiah had come. The Light was there to show the way, Living Water had come to satisfy thirst, and Bread of Life was offered for any who would take and eat.

I came that they may have life and have it abundantly. John 10:10b

6. What phrase is used both in John 11:33 and 11:38 to describe Jesus' emotions?

At just the right time, God, who could have been aloof and distant, came down in the person of Jesus and entered into the pain of His people.

Jesus understood the timing of how things would unfold. He knew the way the story would end even before it started. Lazarus lay cold in the grave, but Jesus knew that even though his story would have to travel through death, it wouldn't end in death. And yet, Jesus wept.

Even though I walk through the valley of the shadow of death, I will fear no evil, for you are with me. Psalm 23:4

Standing at the mouth of an open grave, Jesus knew He would be the One to face the fullness of death in order to defeat it forever. He would absorb death's poison so that those who came to Him for life would only feel its sting. Jesus knew all this, and still, standing at the entrance of His friend's grave, He wept.

> **Hear and give ear; be not proud, for the LORD has spoken. Give glory to the LORD your God, before he brings darkness, before your feet stumble on the twilight mountains, and while you look for light, he turns it into gloom and makes it deep darkness.**
> **But if you will not listen, my soul will weep in secret for your pride; my eyes will weep bitterly and run down with tears, because the LORD's flock has been taken captive. Jeremiah 13:15-17**

Jesus wept because His lost sheep were held captive by the power of sin and death. He wept because He knew they would kill the Shepherd. He wept because, though His people stumbled in darkness, they still struggled to come to the light.

But Jesus did not weep in despair, because — this is the best part — Jesus also knew that being the Good Shepherd who called His sheep by name, He would be able to save them. Jesus would defeat death on the cross with a cry of victory that would echo through time and eternity:

Unbind them and let them go!

Death would not have the last word. Death does not have the last word. When the time is right, our Saviour will return in the twinkling of an eye to swallow up death in the victory He has already accomplished.

> **Fight the good fight of the faith.**
> **Take hold of the eternal life to which you were called and about which you made the good confession in the presence of many witnesses. I charge you in the presence of God, who gives life to all things, and of Christ Jesus, who in his testimony before Pontius Pilate made the good confession, to keep the commandment unstained and free from reproach until the appearing of our Lord Jesus Christ, which he will display at the proper time –**
> **he who is the blessed and only Sovereign, the King of kings and Lord of lords, who alone has immortality, who dwells in unapproachable light, whom no one has ever seen or can see.**
> **To him be honor and eternal dominion.**
> **Amen 1 Timothy 6:12-16.**

Day Two: Chain Reactions (John 11:45-54)

You may have heard the fable about an Arab and his camel. One cold night, as the Arab warms himself inside his tent, his camel sticks its nose inside. The camel is cold and wonders if it could put its head inside the tent to keep it warm. Feeling benevolent, the Arab welcomes his camel to do so.

The camel enjoys the warmth of the tent on its face for a short while. However, it soon notices how cold its neck is. Could it perhaps warm its neck in the tent, as well, the camel asks? "Well, if the head, why not the neck," thinks the Arab, and he allows it.

The night is bitterly cold. The camel's knees knock together making it hard for it to remain standing. The camel pushes its legs through the tent opening, begging its master to be allowed to warm its front legs inside the tent. Less enthusiastically this time, the Arab acquiesces.

Immediately, both the Arab and the camel, realize there is a problem. With half of its body inside the tent and half of its body outside the tent, the night air is allowed in and now both the camel and its master shiver from the chill. The only way to fix this, suggests the camel, is for it to be allowed to move its back legs in as well, thus allowing the Arab to close the tent behind it. This way they both stay warm, the camel reasons.

Unfortunately for the Arab, the tent is too small for both of them and, being the bigger of the two, the camel pushes its owner out.

The moral of the fable is: "It is a wise rule to resist the beginnings of evil."[6] (Scudder, 2017)

Actions have a way of linking together to form a chain, each event tied to the one that came before. As the chain grows thicker and longer, it becomes harder to break. Like a row of dominos which topple with a single push, a chain reaction can crash through a series of individual events that may seem inconsequential on their own, but together result in an epic wreck.

---

[6] Horace E. Scudder, The Book of Fables and Folk Stories, Copyright © 2000-2017 Yesterday's Classics, LLC. All Rights Reserved. www.mainlesson.com accessed November 9, 2017.

Throughout His ministry, Jesus performed signs, all the while pointing people to the substance behind the signs: Himself. Sometimes they didn't see it. Sometimes they saw but didn't understand. Other times, Jesus knew the people both saw and understood, they simply didn't like the implications.

This week we are studying the place in John's Gospel where it seems the chain of action and reaction has grown so strong that things are out of control. It looks like the religious leaders have the upper hand. It appears that Jesus will be forced to run in fear if He has any hope of escaping the danger which awaits Him. The impression might be that the crowd is in control and Jesus' defeat is imminent. But things aren't always as they seem.

1. Read John 11:45-54, using the following questions to guide you through the chain of action and reaction.
   a. What happens as an immediate result of Jesus raising Lazarus from the dead, according to verse 45?

   b. What secondary response is recorded in verse 46?

   c. How do the Pharisees respond to this news in verse 47?

   d. What do the chief priests and officials fear will happen if Jesus is allowed to continue in His ways? (verse 48a)

   e. Why is that a bad thing, according to verse 48b?

   f. What statement does the high priest make in 49b?

   g. How does he further explain it to them in verse 50?

   h. In verses 51-52, how does John explain the words spoken by the high priest?

   i. What plot initiates in response to both Jesus' actions and the high priest's words in verse 53?

   j. How does Jesus respond, according to verse 54?

A series of events is in motion; the contrast between verse 45 and verse 46 reveals that the individuals involved could have chosen to respond differently. They could have broken their link in the chain. They were not pushed along helplessly.

Why did the response from the Jews differ so significantly? Why did some break their connection to the events of the day while others did not? Often response can be attributed to motive, especially when it's from someone with something to lose.

2. Look at verse 48 again.
   a. What two things do the Chief Priests and Pharisees fear will be taken away?

   b. Who will they be taken away from?

   c. Turn to Deuteronomy 7:6. Who does the nation belong to?

   d. Now look at Exodus 25:8. Who does the temple (sanctuary) belong to?

   e. How does the response of the Sanhedrin indicate they had forgotten whose they were?

   f. Why do you think this particular miracle—a man dead four days restored to life—resulted in such vehement rejection from those in power?

Caiaphas, the high priest, believed he was in control and he wanted to keep it that way. The way he saw it, if Jesus was the Messiah, He would have power over the Jews instead of Caiaphas. Fearing he would be replaced, Caiaphas wanted Jesus dead. What's interesting is that Caiaphas seemed to believe the Messiah would have more power than he did, but less than the Romans. Caiaphas was worried that a power struggle would ensue and that the Romans would win. If that happened, the Jews, especially the ruling elite, would lose everything. For Caiaphas, that was definitely bad news.

Caiaphas might have been blind, but he was shrewd, so he proposed a solution: a scapegoat. Pick one person to die on behalf of the many. If Jesus died, the status quo could stay the same. Or so Caiaphas thought.

The idea of a scapegoat wasn't a particularly original idea. Do you remember how in John 7:52, when the Jewish rulers were angry that some of the people were believing in Jesus, they said no prophet comes from Galilee? They were wrong. Jonah came from Galilee. (2 Kings 14:25)

3. Turn to Jonah and read chapter 1.

    a. What was Jonah fleeing?

    b. What natural phenomena occurred to halt his escape plan?

    c. What solution did Jonah propose to save his shipmates?

    d. What solution did God use to save Jonah?

For the fishermen to save themselves, Jonah had to go. The ruling elite in Jesus' day felt the same way about Him. And in the same way the men on the boat thought they could control the fate of Jonah, the Jewish ruling council believed Jesus' fate rested solely in their hands. But to read John 11:45-54 and think that Jesus was swept up in an unstoppable chain of actions and reactions beyond His ability to control is the farthest thing from truth.

Historical Jesus anchored Himself in history because it is His story.

He was not swept along with the tides of human plans and events. He was coming to live out "The Plan." The plan that had been in place since before the creation of the world. It was better for one man to die for the people and He was the man who would die for His people, so that all people could be His people. Jesus did not run from God's plan. He walked resolutely in it and towards it. He did not retreat in fear. He retreated because the timing of His death would be God's, not man's.

When the time was right, the world would see that, while it appeared He spent three days swallowed up in the belly of death, He actually went down in a victory march of proclamation: Life had defeated death! Any chains that bound Jesus were chains that He allowed, so that they wouldn't bind us.

Since therefore the children share in flesh and blood, he himself likewise partook of the same things, that through death he might destroy the one who has the power of death, that is, the devil, and deliver all those who through fear of death were subject to lifelong slavery.
Hebrews 2:14-15

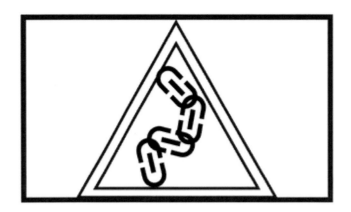

The religious power players thought that when Jesus raised Lazarus from death to life, it sealed His fate and moved Him from life to death. But they were the ones who were bound. They were the ones swept up by chain reactions. Swept away by selfish motives, blind ambitions, and the whims of the crowd, they paved the way for their own death and destruction.

Once again John's Gospel shines its light on us: will we bring the chains that bind us to the only Chain Breaker and allow Him to destroy them? Will we link our chain to His? Or, like the Pharisees, will we be swept away?

He was in the world, and the world was made through him, yet the world did not know him. He came to his own, and his own people did not receive him. But to all who did receive him, who believed in his name, he gave the right to become children of God. John 1:10-12

Day Three: Anointed (John 11:55-12:11)

Dinner parties—love them or hate them? I have a mixed response, one that is closely linked to who is attending. If I don't know the people very well, dinner parties make me nervous. What if the evening is uncomfortable or stilted? Worse yet, what if I do something socially awkward and embarrass myself? (Based on my history, this is a very real possibility.) However, when I know the people well, I love dinner parties. They're an opportunity to enjoy good food, great company, and interesting conversation.

The dinner party we'll read about today is one I would have loved to attend.

1. Read John 11:55-12:8.
    a. What event drew Jesus back into the public eye?

    b. Jesus went to Bethany where a dinner party was held in His honour. Who were the guests in attendance?

    c. Check out either Matthew 26:6 or Mark 14:3—the parallel accounts of this story. Who was the host of this dinner party?

The host of this dinner party was a social outcast—a leper! Characterized by open, oozing, disfiguring sores, leprosy was highly contagious. Doesn't it seem unlikely that this kind of person would be inviting people into his home? And even if he did, wouldn't it seem doubtful that many would attend? We've already read that the Jews were a people known for strict laws regarding cleanliness and purification. At the time this story took place, the Jews were headed to Jerusalem to celebrate the Passover, and they were going early in order to purify themselves before partaking of the Passover feast.

2. Turn back, close to the beginning of your Bible, to Leviticus 13:45-46. How were people with leprosy to conduct themselves, and where were they to live?

3. Read Leviticus 15:31 and Numbers 5:1-3. What was behind the requirement for unclean people to be kept separate from the camp?

4. Now go to Matthew 8:1-4.
   a. What does the man who came to Jesus say to Him in verse 2?

   b. What physical act does Jesus respond with in verse 3?

   c. What does Jesus command this man to do in verse 4?

5. Back to our dinner party, what conclusion do you come to about the current state of the host's condition?

What a dinner party! Presiding at the head of the table was a man Jesus had healed from his uncleanness. Had Jesus not intervened upon his condition, this man wouldn't have been able to interact socially with others, or live in a house in the village, and he certainly wouldn't have been able to have people into his home and eat at a table with them.

Reclining at the table was another man—one who'd spent four days and nights in the bowels of death. When he'd fallen ill, his family had reached out to Jesus, who, instead of running to the rescue had allowed His friend to walk through the valley of death.

And if these guests weren't interesting enough, there was another character at the table. A man who'd walked with Jesus for three years. A man who'd heard His teaching and seen His signs. Judas Iscariot, the disciple who would betray Jesus for only thirty pieces of silver.

Can you imagine what they talked about? The people around the table would have made the dinner fascinating, but what happened while they were eating turned out to be an even bigger deal. At some point while they were reclining around the table, Mary interrupted the evening. She walked in with expensive perfume and anointed Jesus with it. She poured the equivalent of a year's worth of wages on Jesus, and if that weren't hair-raising enough, she wiped His feet with her unbound hair. If there was conversation happening before this, I'm pretty sure it was cut short at this point. Jewish women rarely uncovered their hair in public, and they never allowed it to hang loose.

But Mary didn't seem to be concerned about social convention or norm. She chose to sit at Jesus' feet and learn from Him even though the more traditional role for women was to serve (Luke 10:38-42). Mary had experienced the great love and mercy of Jesus when He'd raised her dear brother from the grave. She didn't care what people thought of her or her actions. She cared far more for Jesus. Mary expressed devotion to Jesus in the most extravagant way she knew how.

6. Read John 12:5-8.
    a. Does Judas' comment in verse 5 seem reasonable on the surface? Explain.

    b. What does John 12:6 show us is the real motive behind the comment?

    c. How does Jesus respond in John 12:7-8?

    d. If you are familiar with Scripture and how the Gospels end, at what point do you think Mary's actions made sense to Jesus' disciples?

7. Read John 12:9-11.
    a. Who enters the scene in verse 9, and why are they there?

    b. According to verse 10, what is the result of verse 9?

    c. Why do they respond this way, according to verse 11?

The dinner party was hosted at the home of a man who'd been cured from what was often an incurable, fatal disease. It was attended by another man who'd been raised from the dead—not maybe dead—four days dead. During the course of the evening Jesus was anointed. Yes, He said it was for His burial, but the people around Him didn't always listen that closely to what He said. And even when they did, they often didn't understand what He was saying. What the people saw, and what they thought they understood, was that this was the anointing of their King.

You see, the dinner party happened during the week of Passover, a time when the Jews—a conquered nation living under the power of Rome—waited for a conquering king, their Messiah, who would come from the line of David. Religious fervour and political tension ran high. Unlike the Jewish leaders who enjoyed their power, the regular Jewish people wanted the status quo to be shaken up.

When the big crowd that witnessed Lazarus being raised from the dead (John 11:19) saw that Jesus was out of hiding and with Lazarus, they couldn't stay away. What kind of army could a man like Jesus raise up if even illness and death weren't barriers for Him? How could any power, even the power of Rome, stand in the way of such a man?

But as much as the regular people wanted a shake up, the religious leaders did not. That's how the same men who were able to justify that one man could be sacrificed for the good of the nation, easily changed that number to two. Willing to do whatever it took to maintain power, they missed the most critical truth of all: the power wasn't truly theirs. They hung tightly to something they were destined to lose, a dangerous position to be in.

8. In Acts 5, Jesus' apostles (including John) found themselves imprisoned because of their Gospel witness, miraculously freed by an angel of the Lord, and interrogated by the council of the Sanhedrin. Read Acts 5:27-39. What conclusion does one of the Pharisees come to in Acts 5:38-39, regarding this situation?

Not one of the events that have unfolded thus far, and not one of the events that are about to unfold, are random or out of control. Each one occurs according to the plan and on the timeline of Almighty God. He is in control. He has the power. Jesus, fully God and fully man, is living out heaven's agenda in perfect obedience without being tossed around by the whims or wishes of man.

That fact is as true of our world today as it was of theirs.

What are you hanging onto, thinking, wishing, or wanting control over? How would it change you to realize that perhaps this very situation has been ordained by God? Does letting go feel easier when you consider that in holding tight you might even be found to be opposing God?

In the beginning was the Word, and the Word was with God, and the Word was God...
And the Word became flesh and dwelt among us, and we have seen his glory, glory as of the only Son from the Father, full of grace and truth. John 1:1, 14

Day Four: Hail to the King! (John 12:12-19)

One of the first times I attended a parade with my children, I got caught up watching the spectacle from their perspective. My children weren't old enough to question what they were seeing, but as I looked at it through fresh eyes, I got to thinking, why would local businesses and organizations put time, effort, and expense into creating a fancy float? Why would they sacrifice hours of their weekend to drive down a parade route, play music, and toss candy at a crowd? Are the powers that be in these companies bored? Are they looking for creative ways to spend excess cash?

I think it's safe to say that the answer to both of these questions is almost always, no. Oftentimes, it seems there's more to do than can be done and never enough money to do it. So why do they do it, then?

For exposure. They want to be seen, understood, and called upon. Colours, music, and decorations are carefully picked so companies can be seen for who they are, understood for what they offer, and called upon as needed. If their message is unclear, this is all lost on the audience.

Jesus enters Jerusalem knowing that a crowd is waiting. He knows what this crowd is looking for. And His message is loud and clear: this is who I am!

1. Read John 12:12-16.
   a. Verse 12 begins with the phrase, "The next day." The next day after what?

   b. What mobilizes this large crowd? (Look at the end of verse 12)

   c. What do the people in this crowd pick up?

   d. What do they call out as Jesus comes into Jerusalem?

    e.   What does Jesus do in response to the crowd's actions, according to verse 14?

    f.   Why does He do this?

We're from a different time and culture than this story is set in, so some of the details are likely lost on us, and their significance along with it.

We already know this parade of sorts is happening during the Feast of Passover. Political and religious fervor, already running high, are escalated by what happened with Lazarus. The crowd that lines the parade route is made up of people who'd seen Lazarus walk out of the tomb, and people who've heard about it from the rumours swirling among Jerusalem's swollen population.

Jesus enters the city to a crowd running high on hope and emotion. Seeing the One who'd raised Lazarus from the dead, they pick up palm branches—the Jewish nation's symbol for victory and kingship—and they start reciting the words of Psalm 118, the final psalm in what is known as the Egyptian Hallel ("hallel" means "praise"). Psalms 113-118 were the psalms Jewish pilgrims sang as they journeyed to Jerusalem for the Passover. They were the songs Jews sang as they remembered their salvation from Egypt on that first Passover, millennia before.

2.   Turn to Psalm 118 and read through the whole psalm.
    a.   What dominant theme is found in verses 1-4?

    b.   Verses 5-18 switch focus. Based on verses 14-16, what would the main theme(s) of this section be?

    c.   Verses 19-29 shift focus again. According to verses 26-29, what is the dominant theme(s) of this section?

    d.   How do you see these themes depicted in the declarations of the crowds who welcomed Jesus into Jerusalem?

People who've been in church culture for a while might hear the word salvation and immediately understand it from our time and perspective on this side of the cross. But to the Jews of that day it meant saving: saving from an oppressive foreign power, saving from the jaws of death, saving through health crises, famine, or persecution. The literal meaning of "Hosanna" is "save now."

When the people saw the sign that he had done, they said, "This is indeed the Prophet who is to come into the world!" Perceiving then that they were about to come and take him by force to make him king, Jesus withdrew again to the mountain by himself.
John 6:14-15

3. Keeping something in Psalm 118, flip back to John 12 and read verses 14 and 15 again. What does Jesus indicate by climbing onto that donkey, and why do you think He now accepts the title?

4. Flip back to Psalm 118 and read verses 19-24 again.
   a. What does verse 21 say Jesus has become?

   b. What has Jesus become, according to verse 22?

   c. Who is given the credit for these things, according to verse 23?

   d. In light of what you've just read above and how the people are interpreting Jesus' entrance into Jerusalem, what day does the crowd think has come and why are they rejoicing in it?

5. Near the end of the Old Testament is the book of Zechariah. Read Zechariah 9:9-10.
   a. How is the coming king described in verse 9?

   b. According to verse 10, what is going to be cut off from the people?

   c. What will the coming king do instead?

The parade into the city of Jerusalem communicated a critical message to all in attendance. For the first time in John's Gospel, Jesus accepts the title, King of Israel. When the crowd meets Him shouting *save now, here comes our king!* He does not correct or rebuke them. In fact, being the source of the Word and knowing His people will know what was written, Jesus not only refrains from correcting the crowd, He reinforces the crowd.

To those lining the parade route, Jesus announces His kingship, while at the same time proclaiming that it will be a different kingship than they are expecting. Their King comes in peace, not war. He comes in a display of humility rather than one of power.

The people shouting for salvation wanted physical and earthly salvation ushered in by a king wearing the victor's crown. But in less than a week, they would see the man they'd proclaimed king wearing a different kind of crown. He would be to them who they needed, not who they wanted. And so, while they looked for physical salvation, Jesus, would show them that their need for spiritual salvation was far greater.

The scepter shall not depart from Judah, nor the ruler's staff from between his feet, until tribute comes to him, and to him shall be the obedience of the peoples.
Binding his foal to the vine and his donkey's colt to the choice vine, he has washed his garments in wine and his vesture in the blood of grapes. Genesis 49:10-11

6. Read John 12:17-19. According to verses 17-18, what two groups of people comprise the crowd?

Some saw with their own eyes. Some heard eyewitness testimony. Many examined the evidence and declared Jesus the king. Were they seeing clearly? History tells us they were not.

History shows us that the same people who were ready to call Him king, were just as ready to crucify Him when He didn't do what they wanted Him to. Yet, Jesus continued to reveal Himself clearly, wanting the people to see Him, know Him, and come to Him for what only He could provide: the salvation of their souls.

The stories we're reading aren't just for entertainment or dramatic effect. From a human perspective, they upset the course of history. From heaven's perspective, they fulfill the course of His story.

How will you respond to this Man who took on flesh and walked among us?

And the Word became flesh and dwelt among us, and we have seen his glory, glory as of the only Son from the Father, full of grace and truth.
For from his fullness we have all received, grace upon grace. For the law was given through Moses; grace and truth came through Jesus Christ. No one has ever seen God; the only God, who is at the Father's side, he has made him known. John 1:14, 16-18

Day Five: Personal Reflection

Pick one or two of the questions below, and journal, pray, or reflect on them.

1. **John 11:33-36 When Jesus saw [Mary] weeping, and the Jews who had come with her also weeping, he was deeply moved in his spirit and greatly troubled. And he said, "Where have you laid him?" They said to him, "Lord, come and see." Jesus wept. So the Jews said, "See how he loved him!"**

   Jesus lived with singular focus: to show God to the world and to show the world that He was God. Here, Jesus is showing us God's love. Do you have a hard time reconciling Jesus' deep love and emotion for His people with your image of God? Explain. Do you believe God loves you this deeply? Why or why not? How does the knowledge that Jesus came to show us the Father deepen your understanding of the character of God? What attributes or character traits of God have you seen illuminated through the person of Jesus Christ?

2. **John 11:47-48 So the chief priests and the Pharisees gathered the council and said, "What are we to do? For this man performs many signs. If we let him go on like this, everyone will believe in him, and the Romans will come and take away both our place and our nation."**

   Acts 5:35, 38-39 And he said to them, "Men of Israel, take care what you are about to do with these men…keep away from these men and let them alone, for if this plan or this undertaking is of man, it will fail; but if it is of God, you will not be able to overthrow them. You might even be found opposing God!"

   Willing to do whatever it took to maintain power, the Jewish religious leaders missed the most critical truth of all: the power wasn't truly theirs. They hung tightly to something they were destined to lose. What are you holding tight to, unwilling to give completely to God? How might an accurate understanding that everything is *from* God and *for* God break the chains that bind, and free you up to live completely for Him and for His glory? Are there ways you are resisting, even opposing, God's leading in your life?

3. **John 12:13-15 So [the crowd] took branches of palm tress and went out to meet Him, crying out, "Hosanna! Blessed is he who comes in the name of the Lord, even the King of Israel!" And Jesus found a young donkey and sat on it, just as it is written, "Fear not, daughter of Zion; behold, your king is coming, sitting on a donkey's colt!"**

   Jesus enters Jerusalem knowing a crowd waits. He knows what they're looking for. His message is loud and clear: this is who I am! But He would be to them who they *needed*, not who they *wanted*. And so, while they looked for physical salvation, Jesus, would show them their need for spiritual salvation was far greater. Do you trust God's sovereignty and plan for your life? Do you trust Him to be who you need, even if it doesn't always look like what you want? What evidence in your life backs up your answer? What would it look like to trust God completely with your life? What steps can you take this week to grow your intimacy and trust in God?

Teaching Session Six: For This Purpose, I Came
(John 12:19-60)

❖ God revealed Himself *to* the specific people He planned to reveal Himself *through*.
  ◆ Jesus came to His people first, because they were the ones who'd been given information about Him, they were the ones waiting for Him, so they were the ones who were most able and prepared to recognize Him.

❖ God doesn't operate according to man's wants. He knows what we need, and what the world needed then and still needs today, more than anything else, is salvation in Christ alone. Salvation is what Jesus promised, and it is for ALL who believe that He is the Messiah, the Son of God.

The Pharisees said to one another, "You see that you are gaining nothing. Look, the world has gone after him." Now among those who went up to worship at the feast were some Greeks. John 12:19-20

❖ Jesus would be glorified in the whole world. Not just the Jewish nation, but the whole world, Greeks included, would see Him.

Truly, truly, I say to you, unless a grain of wheat falls into the earth and dies, it remains alone; but if it dies, it bears much fruit. John 12:24

❖ The only way a grain of wheat can accomplish its purpose and feed people is by first been buried.
  ◆ Glorification will look more like death on a cross than power on a throne.
  ◆ Jesus said: to serve Me, you have to follow Me—even unto death.

❖ What does following Jesus unto death mean for us?
  ◆ We must die to ourselves and our current way of living.
  ◆ We must put to death our desire for power, wealth, self-glorification, selfish ambitions, and the approval of man, and seek Him and His glory alone.

❖ Jesus came to show us the Father (John 1:18) through a life of perfect obedience and submission, even to death. This is how He brought glory to the Father.

And I heard a loud voice in heaven, saying, "Now the salvation and the power and the kingdom of our God and the authority of his Christ have come, for the accuser of our brothers has been thrown down, who accuses them day and night before our God. And they have conquered him (HOW?) **by the blood of the Lamb** *and by the* **word of their testimony, for they loved not their lives even unto death***."*
Revelation 12:10-11

❖ Satan has no more power to accuse those who come to Jesus in faith because the cross stripped him of it.
   ◆ Satan knows he can't accuse us before God, so instead, he accuses us to ourselves and to each other.

❖ Jesus tells them that to defeat the power of sin he has to die…but they understood from Scripture that the Son of Man would reign forever. They were confused. This isn't what they'd signed up for. This isn't what they'd been taught. And so, they doubted He was who He said.

❖ Jesus warns them…the light will only be among them for a little while longer. Walk in the light while you can or darkness will overtake you. When you walk in the dark you don't know where you're going, so walk in the light. While you see the light, believe, become children of light.

❖ Jesus wants the people to recognize that the issue isn't really seeing, but responding. They can see the signs. They can even believe them to be true. But the defining factor is their response. Will they live like this is true?

❖ What if we stopped trying so hard to explain ourselves and focused more on explaining *Jesus*? With actions and lifestyles that backed up our words. What if we took the spotlight off of ourselves and pointed it on Him?!

❖ The seeing isn't actually very hard. It's the following that is.

How will you respond when you hear the words of Christ?

View this teaching session at www.unshakenministries.com

Session Notes:

WEEK SIX: AN EVENING WITH JESUS

Amidst the swirling action of historically-altering chain reactions, Jesus' public ministry on earth is done. He has arrived at the evening that history has been leading up to. But rather than plunge into the final showdown with guns blazing, Jesus steps back and arranges a quiet evening with His closest friends.

Where the first twelve chapters of John's Gospel focused on Jesus' public ministry, the next five chapters shift focus to Jesus' private ministry. There is another significant change starting in chapter 13. During His public ministry, John records Jesus performing signs, then teaching His witnesses the significance of the signs. Chapters 13-17 show Jesus teaching His closest followers in advance. Before they can grasp the most significant sign of all—His crucifixion—Jesus' followers must be prepared.

Jesus knew this night led to the cross. He knew that His humiliation, torture, abandonment, and death would be the most difficult sign of all for His disciples to understand, so He taught them before He showed them.

This night of unfathomable love and unswerving obedience was no ordinary night. Jesus' words are no ordinary words.

This is how it begins:

Now before the Feast of the Passover, when Jesus knew that His hour had come to depart out of this world to the Father, having loved His own who were in the world, He loved them to the end.

John 13:1

Come, spend an evening with Jesus.

> **But to all who did receive him, who believed in his name, he gave the right to become children of God, who were born, not of blood nor of the will of the flesh nor of the will of man, but of God.**
> **John 1:12-13**

Day One: Washing Feet (John 13:1-30)

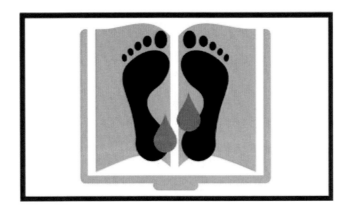

Before you begin today, read the chapter introduction on page 120 to make sure you're well-oriented. Once you've done that, open your Bible to read John 13:1-30.

Is this scene about washing feet?

Clearly that's what is happening in this scene, but is that the point? Do you think John included this beautifully tender and intimate scene as an encouragement to his readers to be willing to stoop down and wash dirty, rough, smelly appendages? Keep this question at the back of your mind as we move through our lesson today.

If you've ever been invited out for dinner, you know it's appropriate to arrive reasonably clean if it is within your ability to do so. But if you've ever had to stop before arriving to fill your vehicle with gas, or maybe buy some flowers for your host, you are familiar with the feeling of being clean but still wanting to wash your hands before sitting down to eat.

In the time and culture this scene takes place, guests would likely have arrived at dinner on foot wearing open-toed sandals. They were clean—except for their feet. Therefore, it was customary for the host to provide a servant who would wash guests' feet as they entered the home.

From reading the account of the Last Supper in the Synoptic Gospels (Matthew 26, Mark 14, Luke 22), we see that Jesus was the host of the meal. That meant He was responsible for making sure there was a servant present to wash the disciples' feet as they came in to eat.

1. Read the first phrase of verse 2 and the first phrase of verse 4 in John 13. Does the foot-washing happen at the customary time?

2. What can you infer about Jesus' intentions from the timing of the foot washing?

I wonder what the disciples thought about the apparent breach in etiquette when they came to share the Passover meal and there was no servant waiting to wash their feet as they entered?

I wonder if it occurred to any of them to do it for each other?

**A dispute also arose among them, as to which of them was to be regarded as the greatest.
Luke 22:24**

The above verse from Luke's Gospel happens in the middle of the same evening — the night of their last supper together when Jesus washed their feet. While the disciples were thinking about how to climb higher, Jesus bent down to get lower.

You see, washing feet was a job that was both despised and looked down upon. There were times a disciple or apprentice might wash their master's feet as a sign of devotion, but there is no record of the order being reversed. Washing feet was typically a task assigned to the lowest of servants. Even Jewish servants considered washing feet to be beneath them and so the task was usually left for Gentile servants to complete. Washing feet was as low as you could go.

And [Jesus] said to them, "The kings of the Gentiles exercise lordship over them, and those in authority over them are called benefactors. But not so with you. Rather, let the greatest among you become as the youngest, and the leader as one who serves. For who is the greater, one who reclines at table or one who serves? Is it not the one who reclines at table? But I am among you as the one who serves. Luke 22:25-27

Clearly, what Jesus did that evening carried great significance. What was behind it?

3. Using John 13:1-30, fill in the chart below making a point-form list of all that we see Jesus knew, and all that the disciples (either as a group or individually) did not know.

What did Jesus know?	What did the disciples not know?
V 1:	V 7:
V 3:	V 22:
V 11:	V 28:
V 18:	

4. We've seen what Jesus knew and that He knew it before the foot washing took place. How does this knowledge add deeper significance to Jesus' actions?

Blessed and holy is the one who shares in the first resurrection! Over such the second death has no power, but they will be priests of God and of Christ, and they will reign with him for a thousand years.
But as for the cowardly, the faithless, the detestable, as for murderers, the sexually immoral, sorcerers, idolaters, and all liars, their portion will be in the lake that burns with fire and sulfur, which is the second death. Revelation 20:6, 21:8

5. Write down Jesus' words in John 13:8. Now look more closely at the exchange between Peter and Jesus in verses 8-11. Using the verses above to help you, what do you think Jesus is saying?

Jesus ultimately tells Peter that if he refuses His washing, he is rejecting Christ, just as Judas has. Peter fearfully responds by asking Jesus to wash all of him. But Jesus, the ever-patient Master and Teacher, gives another lesson in love: *if you've already accepted Me, if you already believe I am who I say I am, then you're clean, covered by My blood. Peter, you are clean, but continue to come to Me daily. Humble yourself before Me in repentance and confession, allowing Me to wash away the stains from daily living so that I can make you whiter than snow.*

Jesus has been ministering publicly to His own people, the Jews, for three years. He has performed signs and then taken the time to teach His witnesses regarding the significance of the signs. He has repeatedly shown them and told them that while He is using physical examples to make His point, His far-deeper concern lies with spiritual realities, not physical.

Teacher:
someone who causes others to learn or understand something by example or experience, one who imparts knowledge, instructs

Master:
a person with the ability or power to use, control, or dispose of something, one with complete knowledge or skill

6. What lessons reveal Jesus as teacher in this chapter? Provide evidence from the text to support your answer.

7. What actions or words of Jesus reveal Him as master in this chapter? Provide evidence from the text to support your answer.

Though He had done so many signs before them, they still did not believe in him. John 12:37

The people did not see, so Jesus shifted His focus on this final night to those closest to Him, those who walked alongside Him during His ministry. He prepared them. Instead of performing the sign and then explaining it, He explains, models, and teaches His disciples to prepare them for the sign that is coming: His betrayal, torture, humiliation, and death.

By the cleansing of their feet, and the cleansing of their community with Judas' departure, Jesus prepares His disciples for the ultimate and lasting cleansing that He would bring through His work on the cross.

That evening, the disciples thought washing feet was about as low as you could go. Jesus would go much lower than that. Knowing all power had been given to Him, He modeled for them profound obedience motivated by love, and He washed the feet of the man who would betray Him. Why?

Because this scene is about so much more than washing feet — it is about the cross!

What I am doing you do not understand now, but afterward you will understand…
I am telling you this now, before it takes place,
that when it does take place you may believe that I am he. John 13:7, 20

8. In what way do Jesus' actions point the disciples to the cross?

Jesus knew the cross would be the most difficult sign of all for them to understand. Jesus knew that the only way up, was by going low. He knew that His triumph on the cross would look like defeat. He knew that while He would be leading a victorious procession into heaven, they would see His body lying cold and dead. Jesus knew that His abandonment would seem like theirs. But He also knew the cross was the only way to fully love them to the end.

Have this mind among yourselves, which is yours in Christ Jesus, who, though he was in the form of God, did not count equality with God a thing to be grasped, but emptied himself, by taking the form of a servant, being born in the likeness of men. And being found in human form, he humbled himself by becoming obedient to the point of death, even death on a cross. Therefore God has highly exalted him and bestowed on him the name that is above every name, so that at the name of Jesus every knee should bow, in heaven and on earth and under the earth, and every tongue confess that Jesus Christ is Lord, to the glory of God the Father. Philippians 2:5-11

Day Two: Where Are You Going? (John 13:31-14:6)

In the passage we looked at yesterday, we saw the small community of disciples being cleansed. Symbolically through the washing of their feet, and physically with the removal of the betrayer from among them.

And then it was night. The darkness that had swirled around them had been held at bay by the light of the world. Soon it would descend in full force—the light would be taken away. The wheels that would turn the course of history had been set in motion.

What an intense scene! We, the readers, know what is happening—we know that Judas left the room to complete his act of betrayal. We don't know exactly how long Jesus has, but we know it won't be long before the betrayer returns. So we lean in as we read John's next words: "When he [Judas] had gone out, Jesus said, 'Now is the Son of Man glorified, and God is glorified in Him.'" (John 13:31)

The disciples have seen a lot! Lame men walking, blind men seeing, dead men coming to life. But Jesus says the greatest glory is still coming—they will see even more glory. Did they understand at the time? No. Jesus taught His disciples that evening knowing many of His words and lessons would be missed, confused, and misunderstood. But He also knew they would echo through eternity. So as the cross loomed, Jesus prepared His followers.

1. Read John 13:31-14:14: After announcing His glorification which will result in glory for His Father, what does Jesus tell the disciples next, in verse 33? What is He preparing them for?

2. That's a pretty big statement, but Jesus doesn't linger long. He moves into the lesson in the next two verses.
    a. What principle does Jesus teach His disciples in verses 34-35?

b. " . . . you shall love your neighbour as yourself: I am the LORD." (Leviticus 19:18) This is the old command from Leviticus. How is it different from the new command Jesus has just given them?

c. Remembering what has just happened, how do John 13:1 and the events of the evening (the washing of feet) model or teach the new command?

The first lesson Jesus wants to teach them is about love.

3. Look at verse 36. Who interrupts Jesus' teaching and what question does he interrupt it with?

Don't you just love Peter?! He's the guy who doesn't know what he doesn't know. *You're never going to wash my feet! What? The only way I can share in you is if you wash my feet? Okay, then don't just wash my feet, wash my whole body!*

Now, sitting around the same table on that same evening, Jesus tells His disciples that He is going away. He starts to prepare them for how they are to conduct themselves in His absence by teaching them more about the love which is supposed to define them. Once again, Peter interrupts the lesson. He backs Jesus up because he needs some clarification. *Where are you going? Why can't I come with you? I will go with you!* Peter's not ready for the lesson on love because he's worried about logistics.

4. What does Peter say to Jesus in verse 37?

5. How does Jesus respond in verse 38? (Feel free to paraphrase)

Peter thinks he's ready to die for Jesus, but it is Jesus who will die for him. Peter thinks he's brave enough to walk the same path as Jesus, but Jesus tells Peter that not only will he run from the path, he will deny the One who defines it.

How do you think the other ten disciples would have felt after hearing Jesus predict that Peter, the man who, after Jesus, was likely their leader, would deny knowing Him? Well, we can infer how they are feeling by what follows.

6. Read John 14:1a.
   a. What does Jesus say to His disciples?

b. Flip back a couple of pages to John 12:27. Knowing what lies before Him, what is Jesus' emotional state?

c. What does John 13:21 say about how Jesus was feeling, and why was He feeling this way?

Jesus is troubled because He knows what's coming. The disciples become increasingly anxious as they begin to comprehend what Jesus says is coming.

Each of them had given up almost everything to follow Jesus: their occupations, their homes, to some extent their families, the favour and good standing of their community. You see, the growing hostility of the Jews towards Jesus would have been reflected onto His disciples, as well. Yet, they still stuck with Jesus, staking their very lives on the fact that He was the Messiah. Now He says He is leaving them and they can't follow. He tells them one of their very own will betray Him, and Peter is warned that he will deny Jesus.

7. What answer does Jesus give to this troubling fear in John 14:1b? What reasons does Jesus give for them to respond this way in verses 2-3?

Isn't the heart of Jesus beautiful? To this motley assortment of men who had just miserably failed the foot-washing lesson, who'd been His closest followers and yet contained a betrayer and a denier, He doesn't offer condemnation but comfort. When Peter interrupts because his head wants details, Jesus addresses the heart's need for consolation. Yes, He is going away, but it is to make a way for them to be with Him, and they know the way.

This is the point where Thomas enters the scene again. Remember the guy who upon hearing Lazarus had died said let's go to him and die with him? Like Peter, he backs Jesus up. *Jesus, if we don't know where you are going, how will we know the way?* Once again Jesus' listeners are focused on physical logistics when He is trying to teach them spiritual truths.

8. How does Jesus answer Thomas in verse 6?

I have chosen the way of faithfulness;
I set your rules before me. Psalm 119:30

9. Based on the words of Psalm 119:30 and the behaviour of the religious leaders throughout this Gospel, what do you think Jewish people understood the way to be? How do you think truth and life would have been connected to the way?

Throughout this Gospel, we've seen that the religious people of the day believed that the way to God was through obedience to His law. They were right. The law led to God. But somewhere along the path of obedience, they lost sight of the fact that the destination wasn't intended to be obedience in and of itself. God's law and obedience to it, was supposed to lead them into relationship with God.

You make known to me the path of life; in your presence there is fullness of joy; at your right hand are pleasures forevermore. Psalm 16:11

In the Old Covenant, God revealed Himself to His people through the physical realities of the law. Sinful humanity could only be in the presence of Holy God by first being cleansed by the blood of a sacrifice, a physical reminder that sin equals death. But, out of love for His people, God allowed a substitute to die in the place of sinful man.

Now even the first covenant had regulations for worship and an earthly place of holiness. . . These preparations having thus been made, the priests go regularly into the first section, performing their ritual duties, but into the second only the high priest goes, and he but once a year, and not without taking blood, which he offers for himself and for the unintentional sins of the people. By this the Holy Spirit indicates that the way into the holy places is not yet opened as long as the first section is still standing (which is symbolic for the present age.) Hebrews 9:1, 6-9a

10. If the law was just a cold set of rules, do you think God would allow a substitute to take the place of the people? Why or why not?

Therefore, brothers, since we have confidence to enter the holy places by the blood of Jesus, by the *new and living way* that He opened for us through the curtain, that is, through His flesh . . . let us draw near with a true heart in full assurance of faith. Hebrews 10:19-20, 22a (emphasis added)

The law was never supposed to be a set of harsh rules followed ritualistically. It was always intended to guide people into relationship with God. The law was always the way for Holy God and sinful man to be together, and it was always pointing to Jesus.

Jesus said to him, "I am the way, and the truth, and the life. No one comes to the Father except through me." John 14:6

The Jews thought the way to God was through the law. Jesus showed them that He was the fulfillment of the law and the only way to get to the Father was through Him.

We might find the disciples' questions and confusion hard to understand. They saw the physical realities: lame men walked, blind men saw, a dead man was raised to life. And all this was done by a physical Jesus. But we can't forget, they also saw Jesus tired, thirsty, hungry, and sad. They believed He was the Messiah, but they also saw Him betrayed, beaten, and killed, and doing nothing to stop it from happening. Can we blame them for sitting huddled together in fear while the Light of the World, the Resurrection and the Life, lay dead in a borrowed tomb?

Their faith was constrained by the presence of a physical man. Ours is anchored by the indwelling presence of the Holy Spirit.

But that's another lesson for another day.

The sting of death is sin, and the power of sin is the law. But thanks be to God, who gives us the victory through our Lord Jesus Christ. 1 Corinthians 15:56-57

Day Three: Show Me Your Glory (John 14:6-14)

Yesterday we were reminded yet again how easy it is to stay stuck on physical realities without moving past them to the spiritual. That lesson is hitting home for me today. My physical reality is that I have a doctor's appointment which I'm dreading. I'll be receiving an injection to prepare my body for surgery in three months. I read the list of side effects for the medication and my heart is troubled. I'm worried that what is supposed to help me might actually harm me first.

I'm trying to learn my spiritual lessons well, so I take my troubled heart to God in prayer. But honestly, right now I want to pray in light of physical realities only. *Save me from embarrassing physical changes, save me from pain, and save me from rare and dangerous side effects that could even end in death.*

Well, wouldn't you know, tucked away in our passage today is a verse that says, "Whatever you ask in my name, this I will do." (John 14:13) Could this be my confidence for today? Could I just ask in the name of Jesus to be saved from all that I fear and know that in three months my body will be healthy and healed?

What do you think? Are any red flags popping up? Let's get into our lesson for today and see if we can come across anything that might help us with this dilemma.

Jesus said to him, "I am the way, and the truth, and the life. No one comes to the Father except through me. John 14:6

1. In John 14:6, what is the way? What is the destination?

We've seen in this Gospel that the Jewish people revered the prophet Moses as a hero of the faith, and claimed to follow God by obeying Moses.

Exodus 32-34 is a fascinating passage in the Bible. The people God had chosen to use to reveal Himself to the world had just made and worshipped a golden calf while their leader, Moses, was on a mountain with God, receiving His law. God was angry with their idolatry and said that, though He would send an angel ahead of them into the Promised Land, He wouldn't go with them. God would give them their physical promise, but He wouldn't be a part of it—the spiritual component of their promise would be missing.

How does Moses respond to this? *Not good enough!* he says. Moses tells God, these are your people, and the only thing that distinguishes us from the rest of the people on earth is that You are with us. (Exodus 33:13-17)

God's presence defines God's people.

God was pleased with Moses' response. God says that because Moses had found favour with Him, He would go with them into their land of promise. And this next part is fascinating: knowing that he had found favour with God, Moses uses the opportunity to ask for something big. He's in a good position to pray the biggest prayer he could have prayed.

Now pause for a minute to consider:

2. If you had been leading God's chosen people—who had already proved to be cantankerous, fickle, and argumentative—into the Promised Land by way of hostile desert tribes and nations, and you knew you had God's favour so it could be a good time to ask for something big, what do you think you would pray for?

I don't know what's on your list, but if I had been Moses, teleportation might have appeared on mine. Not Moses. What Moses asks of God is, "Please, show me your glory." (Exodus 33:18) That was Moses' heartfelt plea and longing. Wow!!

Maybe you're wondering how this ties into our passage in John today, so let's read our portion of Scripture and see how it all comes together.

3. Read John 14:6-14. How does Philip's question in verse 8 echo Moses' words in Exodus 33:18?

4. In your own words, summarize Jesus' answer to Philip in verses 9-11.

5. Based on what you've seen in John's Gospel so far, and also based on John 14:8-11, write down a description of the relationship between God and Jesus, and how they relate to each other.

   a. Read John 17:25-26: what does Jesus say He has done during His ministry here on earth?

b. How does Jesus reveal His Father to the world, according to verse 10-12 in our passage?

> **And the Word became flesh and dwelt among us, and we have seen his glory, glory as of the only Son from the Father, full of grace and truth.**
> **For from his fullness we have all received, grace upon grace. For the law was given through Moses; grace and truth came through Jesus Christ. No one has ever seen God; the only God, who is at the Father's side, he has made him known. John 1:14, 16-18**

Jesus came in the flesh to physically show God to us. But Jesus wasn't coming to show us what God looked like, physically. If you have ever loved deeply, you know that physical appearance means very little where love is concerned. Love grows from knowledge of character—who the person is and how they behave. Centuries before Jesus took on flesh, the prophet Isaiah foretold that, "He had no form or majesty that we should look at him, and no beauty that we should desire him. He was despised and rejected by men; a man of sorrows, and acquainted with grief; and as one from whom men hide their faces' he was despised, and we esteemed him not." (Isaiah 53:2-3)

Jesus came in the flesh to physically show us the character of God—who God is and how He behaves. The people of Israel had seen God's character in the law given through Moses: holy, just, merciful in allowing the price of sin to be paid by a substitute rather than the people themselves. That was the first grace. Now, in more grace, Jesus comes in the flesh. Living out the truth of who God is. Healing the sick, welcoming outcasts, raising the dead. Grace upon grace upon grace. Jesus is speaking the words of God and living out the character of God. And He tells His disciples on this last night before the cross that, though seeing the physical reality of God is hard for them to understand, they could at least believe on account of the works themselves. He challenges them to look to what all the signs have been pointing to.

6. Flip back to John 13:31-32 and then read John 14:12-14 again. We've come full circle today. What connection do you see between these verses? What deeper meaning is Jesus pointing His disciples to in John 14:12-14?

After the golden calf episode of Exodus 32, God told Moses that He would destroy the people of Israel and make a great nation out of Moses. Moses had the opportunity to grab for glory. But he didn't! Instead, he argued with God about this plan. He told God that His glory would be compromised because the nations around them would see the destruction of the people of Israel and think God wasn't powerful enough to bring them through the desert into their Promised Land.

When greater glory for Moses would take glory away from God, Moses wouldn't even consider it. Instead, Moses embraced the more difficult path because it was the path on which God would be most glorified in the world.

At the beginning of His ministry, Jesus is tempted in a desert much like Moses was. The devil takes Jesus to a high mountain to show Jesus all the kingdoms of the world and their glory. And then Satan says, "All these I will give you, if you will fall down and worship me." (Matthew 4:9) Satan offers Jesus a shorter, easier path to power: have it all without suffering the cross. Satan was offering to give his rule of the kingdoms of the world to Jesus in exchange for worship from Jesus. Jesus could have abandoned the difficult way that would lead to the cross, and He could have severed His relationship with the Father to bypass suffering. Instead, He chose pain and death. Instead, He chose to give of Himself so the Father would be glorified.

7.   What greater works do you think Jesus refers to in verse 12?

8.   According to the end of verse 13, why will Jesus do whatever we ask in His name?

I think it comes back to destination. If we're more interested in what's in it for us than we are in being in the presence of the Father, we'll easily trade His glory in for our own. And we'll be seduced into thinking we've made the better trade. We'll celebrate the easy path, lift up physical successes, and be happy with what we perceive as answered prayer, even if the end result is that we are no closer to the One we pray to.

Saying the words might be easy, but what will it be like to live them? Maybe hard. Maybe painful. Maybe confusing, but will I take my troubled heart to Jesus, the One whose heart was greatly troubled on the path to the cross? The One who prayed that the path be taken from Him if possible, but if not, that God's will be done?

Might the greatest thing we can do, be to pray "Thy will be done"?

If you feel like this seems impossibly difficult and not at all doable, you're right. We can't pray like this, believe like this, behave like this, or even desire any of this on our own.

What?! That doesn't sound promising! It isn't. Not if we're left alone to accomplish it. But here's a sneak peek of tomorrow's title: Never Alone.

Take heart today. Don't let your heart be troubled. Believe in God. Believe in Jesus who makes God known. And know that you are never alone.

Let not your hearts be troubled. Believe in God; believe also in me. In my Father's house are many rooms. If it were not so, would I have told you that I go to prepare a place for you? And if I go and prepare a place for you, I will come again and will take you to myself, that where I am you may be also. John 14:1-3

Day Four: Never Alone (John 14:15-31)

Do you remember how in John 13 Jesus started teaching His disciples how to conduct themselves in His absence, and the lesson started with the new command to love each other in the same way that He had loved them?

A new commandment I give to you, that you love one another: just as I have loved you, you also are to love one another. By this all people will know that you are my disciples, if you have love for one another. John 13:34-35

Do you remember how Jesus was interrupted by disciples concerned about logistics and physical location? Well, in our passage today, Jesus circles back to His lesson on love.

If you love me, you will keep my commandments. John 14:15

The problem we were left with as we ended yesterday, was that much of what Jesus was trying to teach His disciples was hard! Too hard to do alone. Jesus knew this. He knew that in their own strength, His followers would continue to fail. That they'd be unable to live up to the standards He set. So He provided a way.

1. Read John 14:15-31. What has been done in answer to our problem?

2. According to verse 16, for how long will the Father give us this Helper?

3. What name is used to describe the Helper at the beginning of verse 17?

4. What do we learn about the character or function of the Helper in the following verses?
   a. Verse 16

   b. Verse 17

c. Verse 26

In John 14:16, Jesus asks the Father to send another Helper to be with His followers forever. The word "Helper" is translated from the Greek word "parakletos" which, in English, has been translated as "helper, advocate, counsellor, comforter, intercessor."

parakletos

Comforter (Consolation of Israel: Isaiah 12:1; 49:13)

Advocate (John 14:16, 26; 15:26; 16:7; 1 John 2:1) one who speaks in our defense; derived from "one called alongside'; one who pleads another's cause before a judge, counsel for defense; an intercessor

Helper (John 14:26)

5. Think of what Jesus just told His disciples. How do you see the Holy Spirit acting as Comforter in verse 17?

6. Read Romans 8:27. How do you see the role of Advocate being played out here?

7. In what way do you see the Holy Spirit taking on the role of Helper in John 14:26?

My dear children, I am writing this to you so that you will not sin. But if anyone does sin, we have an advocate who pleads our case before the Father. He is Jesus Christ, the one who is truly righteous. He himself is the sacrifice that atones for our sins — and not only our sins but the sins of all the world. 1 John 2:1-2 (NLT)

Jesus called the Holy Spirit, who would descend on believers at Pentecost, another Helper (verse 16). While Jesus was with them, He was their Advocate, Helper, Comforter. He was among them as the very Truth of God. He taught them who God is in both nature and action. Jesus was clearly preparing His disciples for the fact that He would be leaving them — but He would not be leaving them alone!

We started our week by reading John 13:1. "…when Jesus knew that His hour had come to depart out of this world to the Father, having loved His own who were in the world, He loved them to the end." The words of Jesus that we've been reading in John 13 and 14 are all grounded in love.

8. Write down John 14:15, then look at verse 21, 23, and 24, and write down the repeated idea.

9. How do you feel about the word 'obedience'? Does it resonate positively or negatively with you?

It's easy to get tripped up on the word 'obedience,' isn't it? We can feel defeated when we read it because it highlights our imperfection. When obedience is the gatekeeper of relationship, it can shut out love. We've seen that with the religious Jews time and again in this Gospel. They made obedience the gatekeeper and had no love—no love for those who didn't obey to their standard, and no love for the One their obedience was supposed to honor. We've also seen repeatedly in this Gospel that this is not the obedience Jesus wanted.

10. Fill in the blanks: If you love _____, you will keep my _____.

    a. Look at the two blanks you filled in. Who/what is our love to be directed towards?

    b. If the love comes first, what will follow?

    c. How does obedience naturally flow out of love? Why is the order important?

    d. Based on all that we've studied this week, do you think Jesus' disciples modelled perfect obedience? What would be one example you would use to support your answer?

    e. Do you think the disciples displayed love for Jesus? What would be something you'd use to support your answer?

The relationship Jesus revealed between Himself and His Father was perfect. Perfect love. Perfect obedience. The relationship between Jesus and His disciples did not model perfect love or perfect obedience because it was a relationship between a perfect party and some very imperfect ones. Jesus knew this, and that is why He promised to send the Helper. Because we need Him. We can't do it on our own, and even with the Helper, we will not do it perfectly. But those who love Christ have an advocate in Him.

The Helper will come to those who love God and they will receive more of Him. He will not come to those who do not love Him, because they don't want what's already been offered, so why offer more?

When obedience is the gate-keeper, you might end up with compliance but it will come from fear, or maybe the desire to manipulate or control. This will never lead to true or lasting peace. You might get an uneasy peace that is achieved or maintained through force or the threat of force, like the peace of Rome John's readers lived in. But that kind of peace is more like power.

In John 14:22, Judas (not Iscariot) wondered why Jesus wouldn't show Himself to the world. If He was really the Messiah, why didn't He reveal who He was to everyone and bring His peace to everyone?

Jesus didn't come to impose Himself on the world. He came to offer Himself for the world.

Jesus knows the hearts of all mankind. Some might want what He can do for them, but they don't really want Him. Maybe they see Him as a genie in a bottle that they can manipulate for their own glory or gain, but they're not interested in His glory. Others choose to go it alone, thinking they know best and don't need His help. The only way these people can have more of Jesus is if He imposes Himself on them. And He could. He has the power to enforce that kind of obedience. But it's not the kind of obedience He's interested in.

Just as Jesus knew some would reject Him, He knew that there would be some who would recognize and receive Him. These people would want more of Him. Jesus knew their love for Him would be imperfect, but He also knew that as their love grew, they'd long to obey more. To these people Jesus sends the Helper, the Advocate, their Consolation. To these people He offers the intimate relationship of abiding. To these people He offers perfect and lasting love.

If you keep my commandments, you will abide in my love, just as I have kept my Father's commandments and abide in his love. These things I have spoken to you, that my joy may be in you, and that your joy may be full.
This is my commandment, that you love one another as I have loved you. Greater love has no one than this, that someone lay down his life for his friends. John 15:10-13

Day Five: Personal Reflection

Pick one or two of the questions below, and journal, pray, or reflect on them.

1. **Teacher: someone who causes others to learn or understand something by example or experience, one who imparts knowledge, instructs.**

   Master: a person with the ability or power to use, control, or dispose of something, one with complete knowledge or skill.

   On Day 1, we considered Jesus' actions in John 13 as both Teacher and Master, and we saw how the disciples responded. How do you personally respond to Jesus as Teacher? How do you personally respond to Him as Master? Do you have difficulty with either of these portrayals of Christ? Prayerfully consider why that is, when both are Biblical.

2. **John 14:1-7 "Let not your hearts be troubled. Believe in God; believe also in me. In my Father's house are many rooms. If it were not so, would I have told you that I go to prepare a place for you? And if I go and prepare a place for you, I will come again and will take you to myself, that where I am you may be also. And you know the way to where I am going." Thomas said to him, "Lord, we do not know where you are going. How can we know the way?" Jesus said to him, "I am the way, and the truth, and the life. No one comes to the Father except through me. If you had known me, you would have known my Father also. From now on you do know him and have seen him."**

   Put the passage above in your own words. Now consider: what defines the Way? How does this define your life, your heart, your actions, your identity?

3. **John 14:26-27 But the Helper, the Holy Spirit, whom the Father will send in my name, he will teach you all things and bring to your remembrance all that I have said to you. Peace I leave with you; my peace I give to you. Not as the world gives do I give to you. Let not your hearts be troubled, neither let them be afraid.**

   How is the peace of Jesus different than the peace of the world? Do you struggle with fear and/or a troubled heart? How does Jesus want you to manage that? Do you struggle with trusting God? Are you able to pray, "Thy will be done?" Why or why not? How does He want you to respond?

Teaching Session Seven: Abiding (John 15:1-17)

❖ Nothing about the night Jesus went to the cross was beyond His plan or ability to control.

Now if Christ is proclaimed as raised from the dead, how can some of you say that there is no resurrection of the dead? But if there is no resurrection of the dead, then not even Christ has been raised. And if Christ has not been raised, then our preaching is in vain and your faith is in vain... But in fact Christ has been raised from the dead... 1 Corinthians 15:12-14, 20

❖ Consumed with love and grace for even the dregs of humanity, Christ chose to walk willingly and purposefully to the cross as the Passover Lamb, the One whose death was the substitute for ours. Does that turn the whole trial on its head? Does it establish Jesus' intent and motivation? Does it proclaim that every word, every action, every sign, was pre-meditated for a specific purpose?

I am the true vine, and my Father is the vinedresser. Every branch in me that does not bear fruit he takes away, and every branch that does bear fruit he prunes, that it may bear more fruit. John 15:1-2

❖ **What made Jesus say He was the true vine?** Song of the Vineyard Isaiah 5:1-7

The vineyard of the LORD Almighty is the nation of Israel, and the people of Judah are the vines he delighted in. Isaiah 5:7

❖ Israel was God's vineyard. The point of a vineyard is to grow vines which produce fruit that can be harvested and enjoyed. Israel failed as the vineyard of God.
  ◆ Jesus turned water into wine. With this sign, He pointed to the fact that the old wine of the covenant of the law had done its work of preparation. The new wine had come. Wine from different grapes. Grapes taken from a different vineyard. This was the wine of the new covenant of grace.
  ◆ The metaphor of the vineyard pointed to Jesus. Justice, righteousness, salvation, would come to the whole world through Him. The true vine was not Israel. It is not the church. It's Jesus.
  ◆ He'll cut away dead branches that don't grow fruit. He'll prune fruitful branches so they will grow more fruit.

❖ **What did Jesus teach about abiding?** They had to *know*, so their fruit would *grow*, and the world would see it *show*.

❖ **What did Jesus want His disciples to know?** To determine that, we need to look at what Jesus knew on this night.
  ◆ Jesus knew what time it was—He worked within the timelines of His Father's plan and submitted to it.
  ◆ Jesus knew where He was going and how He would get there.

- Jesus knew why He was going — His return would glorify His Father and fulfill His purpose as the founder of salvation who would lead many sons to glory.
- Jesus knew what to do before He left — He would teach and prepare the people He had chosen for this very purpose.

❖ **What is our lesson in abiding?**
- We need to understand what we know.
- What's our place, what's our position?
- We are the branches and our job is to abide — to remain firmly anchored in the true vine.
- How do we do that? We nestle into the intimacy of relationship with the True Vine. We get to know His words so that we get to know Him, we make space for His words to abide in us, and we obey His words.
- Abiding in Him means relationship. Relationship means time: time to get to know His words because they reveal who He is, time to chew on His words to uncover their meaning, time to consider the implications of their meaning for our lives.
- People who abide aren't worried about building names for themselves — they're far-sighted, they're looking forward to a reality they can't see yet but one they know is coming. Their own glory means nothing in the face of God's eternal glory.

These things I have spoken to you, that my joy may be in you, and that your joy may be full.
John 15:11

❖ If Jesus is the true vine, and abiding in Him is how we experience fullness of joy, the fullness of it will only come when we know Him fully as we've been fully known.

For now we see in a mirror dimly, but then face to face. Now I know in part; then I shall know fully, even as I have been fully known. 1 Corinthians 13:12

❖ Our experiences here are shadows, reflections of the image but not the fullness of the image itself.
❖ Full joy from abiding in the true vine will come when we see Him face to face, but there is also joy in abiding in Him here, too!
❖ Abiding grows fruit and that's what fulfills our purpose — abiding in Who we know, and what we know about Who we know, will bring fruit.
- The fruit of love, joy, peace, patience, kindness, goodness, faithfulness, gentleness, and self-control.
- Fruit that characterized the life of the True Vine will grow in our lives and become increasingly evident as we abide in Him and His words abide in us.
❖ Abiding in the vine grows us to look more like God, and that's how we show Him to the world.

Session Notes:

_____

_____

_____

_____

_____

_____

_____

_____

_____

_____

_____

_____

_____

_____

_____

_____

_____

_____

_____

_____

_____

_____

_____

WEEK SEVEN: OVERCOMERS

During the course of an intimate evening where Jesus' teaching and action was grounded in the context of Him loving His own to the fullest extent of His love, Jesus used the image of branches abiding in the vine. He held up the privilege of growing fruit for God's glory, and extended fullness of joy from abiding in Him. He said those who would abide in His love would create a community of love.

Doesn't that sound beautiful—almost magical? Doesn't it feel like this should be the place where we stand in a giant circle, hug, and sing in unison before "The End" pops up on a metaphorical screen?

Except we know that's not how it ends. Jesus taught that the greatest love would go as far as laying down one's life and He would soon live that teaching.

As Jesus sums up the vine imagery, we come to John 15:17 and see that it is a transition verse. While love would define relationship within the community of believers, it would not define relationship with the world. And so, while Jesus urged believers to love one another as He loved them, He also warned that the world would hate them like it hated Him.

Jesus' followers would face opposition, so they would need commitment, strength, endurance, and hope—all of which Jesus offered.

Yes, in the world there will be trial and tribulation, but He has overcome the world. And those who abide in Him will also overcome.

> **For from his fullness we have all received, grace upon grace. For the law was given through Moses; grace and truth came through Jesus Christ.**
> **John 1:16-17**

Day One: Not of the World (John 15:17-16:4)

As a middle child, I have gone through life happily sandwiched between two sisters with my only brother as the baby of the family. There's a lot of interesting research linking birth order and behaviour. I'm a pretty stereotypical middle child, and one of the ways this manifests itself is that I'm not at all comfortable with conflict. I'll intentionally avoid dealing with problems in the hope that they'll disappear on their own. If I can't avoid or ignore conflict, I try to make peace. I just want everyone to get along and love each other.

This is why I love the imagery Jesus employs in the first part of John 15: growing in love for Christ and fellow believers while abiding in Christ. This is the reality I wish would define not just relationships between believers, but the whole world. So while I love the first seventeen verses of John 15, I feel somewhat unsettled by the verses that follow.

You see, Jesus follows up His lesson on love and abiding with a warning that Spirit-filled living will not generate the kind of response we expect. Believers' lives should be characterized by the fruit of love, light, and right-living, but the world won't appreciate what the light exposes.

1. Read John 15:17-16:4.
    a. What two contrasting emotions does Jesus draw attention to in verses 17 and 18?

    b. Why does God command His followers to love each other? What is the motivation behind this command? (You can use 1 John 4:8 and John 13:34-35 to help you with your answer.)

    c. As followers of Christ love each other and the world in the name of Jesus Christ, what response should we expect from non-believers and why should we expect it? (verses 18-19)

d. After warning His disciples about what to expect in this world, what does Jesus command of them in verse 27?

Jesus tells His disciples that their job will be to carry on His ministry by testifying to His name and making the Father known. We, like the disciples, are sent by God to do the same. If God is love, how will we make Him known unless we love like He does?

**By this all people will know that you are my disciples, if you have love for one another.
John 13:35**

The world is watching and they should see the love. But Jesus warns that this doesn't mean they'll return the love.

2. According to 16:1 and 16:4, why does Jesus give His followers this warning?

As a conflict-avoiding person, I need this advance warning! If Jesus hadn't been clear about what to expect, I'd probably be busy trying to fix problems beyond my scope and ability to fix, and I'd be tempted to give in to discouragement and despair when my attempts to fix them didn't work.

3. Flip back to John 7:7. Why does the world hate Jesus?

4. What does Jesus say His followers should expect in John 15:20?

5. Read Matthew 5:10-12. This passage comes from Jesus' Sermon on the Mount. Jesus again sets out the expectation that those who follow Him will be persecuted.
    a. What reason does Jesus give in verse 10 for this persecution?

    b. He follows this teaching by saying that those who believe in Him are "the light of the world." (Matthew 5:14) How might righteous living act as a light to the world?

    c. What connection do you see between Jesus' teaching on persecution and His command to be light? Why would Jesus teach the two together?

Indeed, all who desire to live a godly life in Christ Jesus will be persecuted. 2 Timothy 3:12

6. What do you think is behind Jesus' statement in John 16:4, "I did not tell you this at first because I was with you"? What is He saying they should expect once He is gone, and why they should expect it?

As long as Jesus was on earth, He bore the full force of hatred that His witness and teaching brought about. The time had come for Jesus to go away. In His absence, the hatred which had been directed towards Him would now be directed against people who abide in Him, who obey His teachings, and bear His fruit. Anyone who is in Christ should be visible and identifiable by the fruit they bear. This will attract the attention of the world. And if it attracts the attention of the world, it will also attract its hatred.

7.   Glance ahead at John 17:18 and John 20:21. What work does Jesus have in store for His followers?

Jesus' followers will be going out into a hostile world. He's already sounded the advance warning about impending hardship in John 13:19 and 14:29, and He does it again in John 16:1 and 16:4. By telling them what to expect before it happens, He knows that when it does happen, their faith will be strengthened. Yes, they will face certain opposition, but instead of being defeated by it, they will be filled with joy because of it. Joy in the face of conflict and opposition? Is that even possible?

Yes! Yes, it is possible because, though Jesus is leaving His followers, He is not leaving them alone. He is sending a Helper to them.

8.   In John 14:26, how does Jesus say the Holy Spirit will help?

9.   What is the Helper called and what will He do, according to John 15:26?

For a time, God With Us walked among us, testifying to what God is like. When the time was right, Jesus would return to His Father and a new age of revelation would be ushered in through the work of the Holy Spirit. For a time, God incarnate limited His power to the boundaries of human flesh, but God the Spirit would be power released and unleashed. Like a mighty rushing wind, it would not be contained by fleshly boundaries or geographical borders, but would be free to blow on and through all people.

Nevertheless, I tell you the truth: it is to your advantage that I go away, for if I do not go away, the Helper will not come to you. But if I go, I will send him to you. John 16:7

But that's getting ahead of ourselves, as it's a sneak peek from tomorrow. Today, are you wondering how God the Spirit, whom we can't see, could be better than God the Son, who was seen, touched, and heard? Here's a glimpse:

And when they had called in the apostles (which would have included the author of this Gospel, John!), they beat them and charged them not to speak in the name of Jesus, and let them go. Then they left the presence of the council, rejoicing that they were counted worthy to suffer dishonor for the name. And every day, in the temple and from house to house, they did not cease teaching and preaching that the Christ is Jesus. Acts 5:40-42

The apostles in this story are the same men who were confused by Jesus' teaching. Timid men who scattered when Jesus faced the opposition of the cross and hid behind locked doors even after He had risen. But, empowered by the Holy Spirit, these men stood firm in the face of opposition, imprisonment, beatings, and death.

"Fear not, nor be afraid; have I not told you from of old and declared it? And you are my witnesses! Is there a God besides me? There is no Rock; I know not any." Isaiah 44:8

Abiding in the vine will grow fruit. Fruit will get noticed. Getting noticed will result in opposition, hatred, persecution.

If you're a scaredy-cat like me, don't worry. There's hope! Open up your Bible—it's full of stories about people whose lives were transformed when they heard God say, "Fear not!" People whose witness echoes through the ages, bringing glory to the only God, our Rock. People filled with Holy Spirit power—the same power that raised Jesus Christ from the dead.

This kind of power can't be contained to the pages of a book or the lines of a story. It's real. It's available. And through Christ, it lives in each one of us—in me and also in you.

We now have this light shining in our hearts, but we ourselves are like fragile clay jars containing this great treasure. This makes it clear that our great power is from God, not from ourselves.
We are pressed on every side by troubles, but we are not crushed. We are perplexed, but not driven to despair. We are hunted down, but never abandoned by God. We get knocked down, but we are not destroyed. Through suffering, our bodies continue to share in the death of Jesus so that the life of Jesus may also be seen in our bodies.
Yes, we live under constant danger of death because we serve Jesus, so that the life of Jesus will be evident in our dying bodies. So we live in the face of death, but this has resulted in eternal life for you.
But we continue to preach because we have the same kind of faith the psalmist had when he said, "I believed in God, so I spoke." We know that God who raised the Lord Jesus, will also raise us with Jesus and present us to himself together with you. All of this is for your benefit. And as God's grace reaches more and more people, there will be great thanksgiving, and God will receive more and more glory.
That is why we never give up. Though our bodies are dying, our spirits are being renewed every day. For our present troubles are small and won't last very long. Yet they produce for us a glory that vastly outweighs them and will last forever! So we don't look at the troubles we can see now; rather we fix our gaze on things that cannot be seen. For the thing we see now will soon be gone, but the things we cannot see will last forever.
2 Corinthians 4:7-18 NLT

Day Two: Overcomers (John 16:4-33)

I live in a country where hockey is a big deal. We might not be an impressive power-house country like our neighbours to the south, but the fact that we consistently triumph over them on the ice is a source of national pride.

Our two women's hockey teams faced each other in the gold medal game of the 2014 Olympics, and few Canadians seriously considered the possibility of a loss. You can imagine our shock when, with less than a handful of minutes left in the game, we trailed by not one goal but by two!

My sister, an avid hockey fan, was unable to watch the game live. She set her PVR to record it, and determined to experience the game as it had unfolded. She avoided all media and warned everyone she knew about the dire consequences of revealing any part of the game to her before she'd watched it in its entirety.

She sat down to watch, confidently nurturing a spirit of triumph, so was horrified as the game wound down with Canada trailing by two. She'd almost lost hope when, in a flurry of excitement, the Canadians scored to bring the game within one. They managed to tie it up in the final minute and she was momentarily ecstatic—until she realized they now faced the prospect of overtime, maybe even a shoot-out, both of which could be lost. Caught between the prospect of agonizing loss or spectacular victory snatched from the jaws of defeat, she wondered if it would have been better to have lost definitively from the beginning, rather than to have tasted some hope first. Not knowing was almost unbearable.

She called me to talk through the game when it was over. How had I survived, she questioned? I told her that I'd been in the grocery store during the final moments of the game and had heard the outcome before I saw the first puck drop. I'd known all along whether my hope had been well-placed or misplaced.

When the disciples first began following Jesus, they were pretty sure they were backing a winner. They'd heard, with their own ears, the testimony of John the Baptist when he said he'd been sent to reveal God's Lamb to Israel, and that it was Jesus. (1:29, 31) Andrew brought his brother, Peter, to Jesus with the words, "We have found the Messiah." (1:41) Philip brought

Nathanael to Jesus with the same promise. (1:45) When Jesus showed knowledge of Nathanael's whereabouts before they'd even met, Nathanael responded confidently, "Rabbi, you are the Son of God! You are the King of Israel!" (1:49)

As Jesus' ministry expanded from His inner circle, His disciples saw things they knew could only be accomplished by the power of God. Nicodemus, the Pharisee, acknowledged that God was with Jesus. (3:2) People brought their sick to Jesus, knowing He could heal them. (6:2) Word spread so that people came from all over, believing He was the answer to their sick bodies and sicker hearts. (4:42, 50)

The disciples saw opposition against Jesus grow, but even when He told them that a grain of wheat had to fall to the earth and die before it could bear fruit (12:24-25), even when He told them He'd be lifted up on a cross before He'd be lifted up on a throne (12:32-33), they still didn't understand what He was saying to them. He broke the bread to show how His body would be broken for them, and they argued about who among them would be the greatest when they eventually reigned with Him. (Luke 22:24)

They weren't sure about a lot, but they were pretty sure Jesus was the triumphant victor.

I am telling you this now, before it takes place, that when it does take place you may believe that I am he. John 13:19

And now I have told you before it takes place, so that when it does take place you may believe. John 14:29

I have said all these things to you to keep you from falling away. John 16:1

Jesus knew things were going to get a lot more confusing before they became clear, so He prepared His disciples ahead of time. He didn't want them to lose heart, to lose hope, or to worry that they'd backed the wrong team. Jesus wanted to equip His followers with knowledge so that they would have confidence.

Let's turn to our passage for today and see how Jesus prepared His team before battle.

1. Read John 16:4 and look back at question 6 from yesterday's homework. Why was it crucial that Jesus' disciples understand His warnings now that He would be leaving them?

When Jesus was with His followers, the hatred of the world was directed against Him; His presence was their protection. When Jesus was with His followers, their lack of understanding was met by His teaching; His presence kept them from getting lost in confusion. Now the time had come for Him to leave them, but He wouldn't leave them alone.

2. Read John 16:5-11. Jesus is going away and, understandably, this causes His followers to feel sad. What words does Jesus leave His friends in order to comfort them?

3. Help is on the way! According to John 16:8, what one specific thing will He do?

4. Now break down that one specific action: what three areas will the Helper address, according to verse 8b?

I told you that you would die in your sins, for unless you believe that I am he you will die in your sins. John 8:24

    a. Using Romans 3:23, what do you think the Holy Spirit will help us understand about our sinful nature?

For our sake he made him to be sin who knew no sin, so that in him we might become the righteousness of God. 2 Corinthians 5:21

    b. Using Philippians 3:8-9, what do you think the Holy Spirit will help us understand about our own righteousness?

Now is the judgment of this world; now will the ruler of this world be cast out. John 12:31

    c. Using Colossians 2:13-15, what will the Holy Spirit remind us about judgment and the prince of this world?

    d. How do you think a proper understanding of sin, righteousness, and judgment would help prepare the disciples, and you and I, as well, to carry on the work of Christ after His departure?

The times of ignorance God overlooked, but now he commands all people everywhere to repent, because he has fixed a day on which he will judge the world in righteousness by a man whom he has appointed; and of this he has given assurance to all by raising him from the dead. Acts 17:30-31

5. Read John 16:12-24. What does Jesus say they will feel at first, and what will that feeling be turned into? (verse 22)

6. Read John 16:25-33.
    a. What do the disciples say that they know in verse 30?

    b. What do they believe because of what they know?

    c. How does Jesus respond to them in verse 31-32a?

Jesus warns them that before they will know fullness of joy, they will know deep sorrow — but their greatest sorrow would become their greatest joy when they understood. He knows they are confident they've backed a winner, but warns that before they witness the spectacular triumph, they will taste bitter defeat. They will abandon Him and scatter. They will think the game has ended and their team has lost. And, just maybe, they will wonder if getting so close to victory before having it snatched away is more bitter than having never glimpsed it to begin with.

If you're Canadian, or a hockey fan, you know how the 2014 Olympic gold medal game ended. You know that, though Canada came very close to defeat, they won in overtime.

I knew this before I sat down to watch the game. Because I'd been confident in the ending, I watched the game differently than my sister did. While she battled despair over apparent defeat, I maintained hope. I didn't lose my head during the closeness of the battle. In fact, I relished it. I knew coming so close to losing would make winning sweeter.

Jesus knew that the world would throw its best at His followers. He knew there would be times when the victory would seem out of reach. But Jesus also knew the ending.

nikao
nik-ah'-o
to subdue; conquer, overcome, prevail, get the victory; when one is arraigned or goes to law, to win the case or maintain one's cause

7. Okay, this is a long list, but take heart. You'll quickly see a pattern emerge once you start. Look at the following references: Revelation 2:7, 11, 17, 26; 3:5, 12, 21.

a. What word in each verse comes from the Greek word "nikao"?

b. How do Revelation 12:11 and 21:7 echo what was said in each of the references above?

c. In all of the verses from question a and b, who is the word nikao used in reference to?

d. In Revelation 3:21b, the word nikao is used a second time. How is that use echoed in Revelation 5:5 and 17:14, and what is it pointing to?

We've seen that the word "nikao" is used many times in the book of Revelation—the book that tells us how this story ends. But the only time it's used in John's Gospel is in this verse, John 16:33, on the night before Jesus faces the cross. The night He encourages His disciples to take heart because not all is as it seems. The prince of darkness is defeated. Jesus wins!

Don't look to the defeated world for peace. Look to the One who defeated the world for His kind of peace. That's the kind of peace you can both fight in and rest in when the battle rages.

If you're walking through difficult times, you might worry that by putting your hope in Him, you've misplaced it. If you need your confidence bolstered, finish today by reading a bit from the end of the story, and take heart.

Then one of the elders said to me, "Do not weep! See, the Lion of the tribe of Judah, the Root of David, has triumphed...Then I looked and heard the voice of many angels, numbering thousands upon thousands, and ten thousand times ten thousand. They encircled the throne and the living creatures and the elders. In a loud voice they sang:
"Worthy is the Lamb, who was slain,"
Then I heard every creature in heaven and on earth and under the earth and on the sea, and all that is in them, singing:
"To him who sits on the throne and to the Lamb be praise and honor and glory and power for ever and ever!" Revelation 5:5, 11-13

Day Three: Jesus Prays Part I (John 17:1-8)

Today we study a prayer of Jesus that is, by far, His longest prayer recorded in any of the Gospels. More than that, it's a prayer He prayed on the night His earthly ministry reached its climax. His human form would soon be subjected to the same end all people must face: death.

Jesus' words on this night are precious and rich, so sit up tall, arm yourself with a good cup of coffee (strong and dark is how I like mine), and grab a pen. You won't want to miss this!

1. Read John 17:1-8.
    a. Chapter 17 begins with, "When Jesus had spoken these words." What specific words had Jesus spoken immediately before looking up to heaven to pray? (John 16:33)

    b. Consider Jesus' bold declaration in this verse: "But take heart! I have overcome the world." What is Jesus telling His disciples here?

    c. With these triumphant words in mind, what mood or tone do you think would characterize Jesus' prayer?

2. With what title does Jesus refer to the One He is praying to? (17:1) Peek ahead. How does He expand on this title in verses 11 and 25?

Jesus knows the cross looms. But does He approach it with resigned fatalism? No! There is no despondency or defeat! Jesus looks ahead with the full confidence of assured victory. Does He shrug His shoulders because His course is set and there's nothing He can do about it, so why bother praying? No! Even with an outcome that is sure, Jesus still sees the necessity of drawing strength from His Father, whom He loves and whose love He is confident in. Though Jesus enjoys the intimacy of calling God His Father, He also knows that God the Father is holy—high and exalted—and righteous.

On the night before the cross, Jesus acknowledges the closeness, the power, and the rightness of God!

3. Jesus approaches His Father in confidence. Knowing His time has come, what is Jesus' primary concern at this point? What request does He make in the last part of verse 1?

   a. How will both the Father and the Son be glorified, according to verse 2?

   b. How does Jesus define eternal life in verse 3?

God's glory was Jesus' greatest desire that night. It's the only reason He asked for His own glorification. It was the purpose driving everything Jesus did. As the sent One, Jesus was dedicated to perfect obedience. He had been given authority to accomplish God's eternal purposes and plan, and part of the plan was to give eternal life. Jesus came as the Word made Flesh, the Light of Life in the darkness of death.

When an educated Pharisee came to Jesus in the darkness of night searching for light, he was offered eternal life. (3:14-16) A Samaritan woman living in desperate thirst for love, acceptance, and belonging, was approached by Jesus with an invitation to drink from the water of eternal life. (4:13-14) Religious leaders who'd dedicated themselves to walking by the light of the Law failed to see the One who was the radiance of it, so Jesus offered to open their eyes to abundant and eternal life in Him. (5:24, 10:10)

For I have not spoken on my own authority, but the Father who sent me has himself given me a commandment – what to say and what to speak. And I know that his commandment is eternal life. What I say, therefore, I say as the Father has told me. John 12:49-50

Jesus came to people in all kinds of darkness and offered them the light of life. Eternal life.

4. Quick review: using John 17:3, sum up eternal life in two words.

For the earth will be filled with the knowledge of the glory of the LORD as the waters cover the sea. Habakkuk 2:1

5. How does Jesus say that He brought glory to God in John 17:4?

6. What was He sent to do, according to verse 6? Use John 1:18 to support your answer.

Jesus came to reveal God. Eternal life is knowing God.

If we stop and think about these two statements for a bit, we can see there is a fearful implication in them. John 1:18 says no one has ever seen God. If we cannot see God, we cannot know God. Apart from God we cannot know life. The greatest fear people face is the fear of death. Death is unavoidable, so our fear of it is real.

The story did not start this way, though. God created Adam and Eve and breathed His breath of life into them. They walked with God in the Garden of Eden; they knew God, they had life. (Genesis 3:8) But then they sinned and everything changed. Their eyes were opened to their nakedness. They tried to hide from God by covering themselves with leaves. Their assessment of the situation was accurate but their solution wasn't adequate.

They couldn't cover themselves, but God could. He covered them with the skins of an animal that day. Death crept in on the heels of sin, and mankind could no longer live in God's presence. Humanity was separated from God and disconnected from the only true source of love or life. Because of sin, they faced the fearful and dark predicament that they had come from dust and would one day return to it.

It could have ended there. But it didn't.

Creation has run from its Creator ever since the first glimpse of its nakedness; He has pursued us in love, ever since.

After the account of humanity's rebellion against God in the third chapter of Genesis, there are 1186 more chapters of recorded Scripture. More than one thousand chapters to record God's pursuit of man. In them, you'll read again and again how people ran from God and got into serious trouble because of it. You'll read how God patiently revealed, rescued, and redeemed. How He entered into the mess to say *this is who I am*.

He showed them who He was because
He knew that who He was, was what they needed.

To people desperately lost in the darkness of sin, God sent His Son, Jesus, and said, *look at Him. This is who I am*. With God, "revelation" goes hand in hand with "redemption." Why? Because we all need saving and He alone can save us.

And those who know your name put their trust in you, for you, O LORD, have not forsaken those who seek you. Psalm 9:10

7. What is the implication of knowing, based on Psalm 9:10?

8. What does Jesus say of His disciples and their response to Him in John 17:6-8?

9. Based on what you know of the disciples and how they behaved, even on His last night with them, do you think Jesus is being kind or generous in His assessment of them? Why or why not?

The twelve men closest to Jesus were very imperfect. They were slow to understand, selfish in motive, limited in vision. And yet, in all their confused imperfection, with all that they missed, what all but one of them did understand and accept, was that Jesus was who He claimed to be: God's sent One. Though imperfect, they knew who Jesus was, and it changed everything.

They had been eyewitnesses to the hostility Jesus faced and because He was leaving them, they'd been told it would now be directed towards them. Their greatest fears would soon become more terrifyingly real than they could have imagined.

They would be shaken up, but they would not be shaken loose. Why? Because after those long dark days when it seemed like death and fear had won, life would break through the darkness. Jesus would overcome. They would see that though, the glory of man is as short-lived as the glory of grass or flowers, the glory of God is eternal.

They would be eyewitnesses to the full spectrum of love—love that endured the horrors of the cross to defeat death, love that had nothing to do with who they were, and everything to do with who He is! Love that knew their fears and doubts and failings. Love that was fully acquainted with their secrets and sin. But love that went to the cross anyway. They would be eyewitnesses to the incomprehensible love of God in Christ Jesus!

Our God possesses all the power and all the glory, and still He took the limitations of human flesh upon Himself to show us the fullness of His glory and the sureness of His love. He invites us to stop running from Him and instead, run to Him so we can know Him and live in relationship with Him. Forever.

For now we see in a mirror dimly, but then face to face. Now I know in part; then I shall know fully, even as I have been fully known. So now faith, hope, and love abide, these three; but the greatest of these is love. 1 Corinthians 13:12-13

Day Four: Jesus Prays Part II (John 17:9-26)

Love has captured the imagination of our culture. (Ironically, I am writing this on Valentine's Day!) Love wins! Love appears to be the highest and noblest motivation we can be driven by and it's held up as the ultimate source of unity. A quick scan through social media delivers the message that love without limits is what will transform individuals and change the world. United in love, we'll become better people.

But this trip through social media also led me to places where the same people calling for unconditional love were unlovingly berating people. It seems their love has conditions, after all, and it got me wondering, can there be such a thing as love that isn't anchored in or by anything? Could a love that isn't anchored in right fear be just as fearsome as fear that isn't grounded in love? It's something to chew on as we move through our study today.

As we pick up in John 17, we see Jesus shift from praying for Himself—that He would glorify God—to praying for two different groups of people. Let's take a look at who He is praying for.

1. Read John 17 in its entirety before focusing in on verses 6-19.
    a. Who does Jesus say He is now praying for in verses 6-9?

    b. Why is He praying for them, according to verse 11?

    c. What is He praying for them?
        i. Verse 11 (two things)

        ii. Verse 13

        iii. Verse 15

        iv. Verse 17

d. In verse 18, Jesus gives another reason He is praying for them. What is it?

Jesus divides the world into two: those who are His and those who are not — the divide is sharp, but it doesn't need to be permanent.

The disciples could see that this divide came with a dilemma: they would no longer be of the world, but they would still be in the world. A world which would become as hostile towards them as it had been towards the One they followed. This carried fearful implications because Jesus' disciples weren't directed to hang around, crossing off days on a calendar until He came back and brought them home. They followed the One who had been sent into the world and they, too, would become sent ones.

2. According to John 17:17, 19:
    a. How were they to accomplish their mission?

    b. Define the word "sanctify."

    c. What relationship do you see between "sanctification" and "truth"?

Jesus started out with twelve disciples. We already know that one of them had not only deserted Jesus, but he was also going to betray Jesus.

3. In large part, your answer to this question will be speculation, but what factors do you think drove Judas into this course of action?

Judas had been with Jesus throughout His earthly ministry. He had watched Jesus engage with the world He'd come into. He had witnessed Jesus enter into the need of humanity: the sick were healed, the blind could see, and the dead were raised. Those who came to Jesus crippled, diseased, and distracted, were offered release.

Jesus was in their world, but He was set apart for heaven's purpose. Their darkness did not envelope Him — He shone light into it. Their sickness did not infect Him — He brought healing to it. Their sin did not ensnare Him — He offered freedom from it.

Judas had been chosen out of the world, but somewhere during the course of his three years with Jesus, he decided he wanted back in. Scary thought, isn't it? At some point, he decided the glory of man was a more worthwhile pursuit than the glory of God. At some point, his fear of

God was eclipsed by fear of man. Somewhere along the way, his love for the passing things of this world eclipsed his love for what would last forever.

4. "[Set them apart] (for holy service to God) in the truth; your word is truth. As you sent me into the world, so I have sent them into the world." (John 17:17-18) How were the disciples supposed to be going out into the world, according to this verse?

Before the disciples were sent into a hostile world on mission, Jesus prayed that their unity of purpose would be protected. The only way His followers could safely go into the world on mission was grounded in truth. The truth of God's word. The truth of the identity of the Word. Unity did not trump truth and was never to be at the expense of truth. Rather, unity was to be found in truth.

Judas could not safely be sent out on mission because he was not grounded in the truth. He had rejected the One God sent into the world to reveal who God was.

5. Jesus is not finished praying yet. Let's turn our focus to John 17:20-26.
    a. Who is Jesus praying for in this portion?

    b. What specifically does He pray for in verse 21?

    c. Why does He ask this, according to the end of verse 21?

    d. Summarize verses 22-23.

Isn't verse 20 exciting?! On the night Jesus went to the cross, He prayed for us! And the fact that we're sitting here today studying God's Word is evidence of the effectiveness of the disciples' mission. Jesus was confident that those eleven men who'd gotten it wrong at least as often as they'd gotten it right, would be effective in the mission He sent them on.

Carried along by the powerful Spirit of God, the world has been turned on its head by followers of Christ. For two thousand years the prince of darkness has been trying to put out the light of Christ and yet the church of Christ still stands! This is evidence of the unity of purpose and mission among followers of Christ who have stood on the truth!

The mission of the first disciples has become ours. We, too, are sent into a world that we are to be set apart from. Being in the world means we're susceptible to two temptations: to compromise or to disengage. As the way, the truth, and the life, Jesus did neither. As His sent ones, we are to do the same. But to live this out, it's essential that we are grounded in truth and purposeful in our pursuit of Him. How can we be effectively set apart for God's purposes if we don't know who He is? How can we know who He is apart from knowing His Word?

6. How might love apart from truth, transform love into a fearful thing? How could a right fear of God informed by the great love He showed us in Christ Jesus, reveal that love anchored in truth casts out fear?

Love that is not grounded in, or informed by truth can become a fearsome thing. Love separated from its source will eventually show itself not to be love because true love can't be separated from truth.

7. Read John 17:24-26.
    a. What does Jesus desire?

    b. Why does He desire this?

    c. What will unite followers of Christ throughout time and eternity?

Christ followers will be united, not by eagerly looking for the lowest common denominator of shared ideas, but by abiding in Christ and the fullness of who He is.

That's why everything hinges on who Jesus is. If He is not who He claimed to be—the very revelation of and manifestation of God—then all those who claim to follow Him are as mistaken as He was. Their mission was, is, and will be, as hopeless as that of a deluded man who died on a cross. The end.

But if Jesus is who He claimed to be, then sit up and take notice, because redemption hangs on this revelation. If the man who died on the cross was not deluded, if He was not just a man but was in fact God, then when He blew open that tomb, everything changed! Then every word He spoke has eternal significance, so we would do well to know them. To stand on them. To live by them.

Are we sent into a world that is hostile to our mission because it is hostile to the One who sends us? Yes. But take heart. Jesus prayed that God would be glorified. He prayed that His disciples would be protected, sanctified, and unified. He prayed that one day they would be with Him forever.

God will be glorified. If you are in Christ, you will be protected and sanctified. His church, visible and invisible, is united by abiding in Him. It can declare with confidence that, united with Christ, they will one day abide with Him forever and see the fullness of His glory.

Now to him who is able to keep you from stumbling and to present you blameless before the presence of his glory with great joy, to the only God, our Saviour, through Jesus Christ our Lord, be glory, majesty, dominion, and authority, before all time and now and forever. Amen
Jude 24

Day Five: Personal Reflection

Pick one or two of the questions below, and journal, pray, or reflect on them.

1. **John 13:35 By this all people will know that you are my disciples, if you have love for one another.**
   2 Timothy 3:12 Indeed, all who desire to live a godly life in Christ Jesus will be persecuted.
   Psalm 9:10 And those who know your name put their trust in you, for you, O LORD, have not forsaken those who seek you.

   We are called to love like Jesus loved. Our lives should produce fruit—visible manifestations of His presence in us. Yet, we're warned this type of living will bring hatred and persecution. What holds you back from loving as Jesus did? How has your desire to be accepted by others compromised your mission to make Him known? How are you actively seeking to know Him? What would change if you lived by the words Jesus spoke?

2. **Acts 5:40-42 And when they had called in the apostles, they beat them and charged them not to speak in the name of Jesus, and let them go. Then they left the presence of the council, rejoicing that they were counted worthy to suffer dishonor for the name. And every day, in the temple and from house to house, they did not cease teaching and preaching that the Christ is Jesus.**
   2 Corinthians 4:7-18 (NLT) That is why we never give up. Though our bodies are dying, our spirits are being renewed every day. For our present troubles are small and won't last very long. Yet they produce for us a glory that vastly outweighs them and will last forever! So we don't look at the troubles we can see now; rather we fix our gaze on things that cannot be seen. For the thing we see now will soon be gone, but the things we cannot see will last forever.

   The apostles in Acts were the same men confused by Jesus' teaching in John. Timid men who scattered when Jesus faced the opposition of the cross, and who hid behind locked doors after He'd risen. But, empowered by the Holy Spirit, they stood firm in the face of opposition, imprisonment, beatings, and death. Do you believe the Holy Spirit could work this same transformation in your life? Why or why not? Is it hard for you to live out Paul's attitude in 2 Corinthians? Why or why not? How might this attitude bring joy?

3. **John 14:29 And now I have told you before it takes place, so that when it does take place you may believe.**
   John 16:1 I have said all these things to you to keep you from falling away.

   Jesus knew things were going to get more confusing before they became clear, so He prepared His disciples ahead of time. He didn't want them to lose heart or hope—to worry they'd backed the wrong team. Jesus wanted to equip His followers with knowledge so they'd have confidence. Has lack of knowledge or understanding of Scripture caused you to lose heart and hope? How would a foundational knowledge of truth encourage victorious living? Do you live each day with full confidence of victory? If no, why not?

Teaching Session Eight: On Trial (John 18-19:16)

❖ God's ways are not our ways. His plans don't always seem clear or even good at first glance, and it can be hard to trust when we don't understand.

❖ Was this the plan? If so, could the players in the story trust it? Were they willing to surrender their plans for His?

❖ **Simon Peter**
 ◆ The leader of the disciples, after Jesus.
 ◆ Jesus changes his name from Simon to Peter (or Cephas, which means rock).
 ◆ When Jesus tells Peter that Peter will deny Him, Peter boldly and confidently contradicts Jesus. Peter thinks he's strong enough to stand on his own.
 ◆ He comes into this situation thinking he has control over the plan and that if he gives it everything he's got, it'll be enough.

❖ **John**
 ◆ The beloved disciple who was content to remain in the background.
 ◆ Jesus called John and his brother James, Sons of Thunder.
 ◆ The brothers ask to each sit at Jesus' side in His glory. (Mark 10:35-37)
 ◆ John tries to stop someone from casting out demons in the name of Jesus because he wasn't part of their group of followers. (Luke 9:49)
 ◆ The brothers ask Jesus if they should call down fire from heaven to consume the people who didn't receive Him. (Luke 9:54)
 ◆ Doesn't it sound like calm, quiet John has visions of manipulating the plan just like Peter?

❖ **Judas**
 ◆ He betrayed Jesus with a kiss.
 ◆ He was a thief. He was in charge of the disciples' moneybag and he helped himself to what was in it.
 ◆ He was near Jesus, and he knew Jesus, but was unchanged by his knowledge and proximity.

❖ **Annas/Caiaphas**
 ◆ Joseph Caiaphas was the high priest, and he was a son-in-law to Annas, whom the Romans had appointed to the position of high priest in 6 AD.
 ◆ This family was known for being big, wealthy, powerful, and greedy.
 ◆ The family of Annas and Caiaphas belonged to the Sadducees, who believed that they should be the ruling elite.

View this teaching session at www.unshakenministries.com

- Sadducees didn't believe in the resurrection of the dead so, after Jesus raised Lazarus from the dead, Caiaphas spearheaded, with increased intensity, the plot to have Jesus killed.
- Caiaphas was the one who said it was better for one man to die for the people rather than have the whole nation perish. He wasn't willing to have his beliefs questioned or challenged. He wanted opposition to his beliefs destroyed.
- He didn't care about anyone else's plan. He had his own.

- ❖ **Pilate**
  - He was the Roman Prefect whose primary responsibility was to maintain law and order.
  - Pilate was one of the most hated representatives of Roman rule in the land of Israel because he was known to intentionally antagonize the Jews.
  - He couldn't care less about the plan. He just wanted what was in it for him: power, prestige, and glory.

And he came out and went, as was his custom, to the Mount of Olives, and the disciples followed him. Luke 22:40

- ❖ On the night He knew He'd be betrayed, Jesus took His followers to "their place." His betrayer knew to look for them there.

Then Jesus, knowing all that would happen to him, came forward and said to them, "Whom do you seek?" John 18:4

- ❖ Instead of waiting for His pursuers to come to Him, Jesus went out to meet them.

O Lord our God, other lords besides you have ruled over us, but your name alone we bring to remembrance. Isaiah 26:13

- ❖ Somewhere along the way, the Jewish people forgot who their King really was. Many forgot they even had a king at all.

- ❖ God is in control of every minute detail of every single life. Every part of every moment is within His plan.

- ❖ We can respond in callous ignorance and defiance, we can disregard His plans for our own, we can hopelessly wonder if there even is a plan, or we can come to varying degrees of knowledge or closeness to Jesus but end up deciding that whatever we've got going on is better than what Jesus offers. OR we can respond like Peter and John. With imperfect understanding but stumbling towards Jesus rather than from Him, knowing that what He offers is better than anything and everything we have going on, surrendering our plans to His.

View this teaching session at www.unshakenministries.com

Session Notes:

WEEK EIGHT: MY LORD AND MY GOD!

We have arrived at our final week of homework in the Gospel of John. I invite you, one last time, to come and see: love, obedience, worship, power. Come and see a King on a cross, in a tomb, defeating death. Come and see the One who invited all to come and see that He is who He claimed to be.

To see is to respond. You could possibly respond with indifference, or maybe disbelief. But my prayer is that your response will join with voices echoing throughout the ages as they cry out, *"My Lord and my God!"*

If this is your cry, in some soft, maybe small way, you will hear His voice bid you to go and tell. That might not mean anything for you logistically. There's a good chance you'll stay exactly where you are physically. But as you abide in Him and grow in obedience, you'll find the Light of the world shines bright through you, and people in your life will see. And when God is seen, nothing stays the same.

> **And the Word became flesh and dwelt among us, and we have seen his glory, glory as of the only Son from the Father, full of grace and truth.**
> **John 1:14**

Day One: That Scripture would be Fulfilled (John 19:16-42)

And the Scripture, foreseeing that God would justify the Gentiles by faith, preached the gospel beforehand to Abraham, saying, "In you shall all the nations be blessed."
Galatians 3:8

The months I spent waiting for the birth of our first child were filled with nervous excitement. Because I rightly suspected that I was unprepared for what lay ahead of me, I made an effort to learn as much as I could. I read books, I signed up for email updates, and I peppered other moms with questions. The question I asked most was, "How did you know when it was time?" I wanted to know from people who'd been there which signs I should be watching for. No matter who I asked, the answer was the same: a soft smile and a vague, "You'll know." That answer didn't satisfy me at the time. But when my first labour pain hit, I finally understood.

Rob and I were at our neighbour's house enjoying a barbeque when a sudden, incredible pain gripped my stomach. He was out by the grill and I was in the kitchen, so the second it passed, I shouted loudly for him. I was almost two weeks overdue at this point, so when Rob heard my call, he came running.

When Rob saw that I looked as normal as could be expected, considering the situation I was in, he relaxed and decided to continue with his meal. Though I begged him to take me home, he calmly reminded me that home wasn't more than 20 feet away, and that he would be there as soon as he finished eating. I walked home alone in tears, worried that I would deliver our baby alone on the living room floor while he ate steak a stone's throw away. Rob came home less than an hour later and he wasn't surprised to find me still with child. But what I knew and he did not, was that the baby was coming.

This all transpired during the late afternoon hours on a Friday, and our son was born just before 3:00 in the afternoon on Sunday. Those were long days for us. Fearful, painful, confusing days. But days that culminated in the miracle of new life. As I looked back over the months, weeks, days, and hours of uncertainty and anxiety, I could see how signs, spread apart over the course of time, pointed to a sure outcome. Hindsight can be a beautiful thing.

Events on the Kingdom calendar have been compared to childbirth. They may start slow and seem ambiguous at first, but the closer they come to fulfillment, the more they increase in speed and intensity, and the clearer they become.

Today, we will zoom in on one of these events. A story full of life and beauty all on its own. But viewed through the lens of our passage in John, it's a story that opens our eyes to the One all the signs of Scripture point to.

1. Begin today by reading John 19:16-37.
    a. There is a phrase repeated four times, with variation in wording, in this passage. You'll find it in verses 24, 28, 36, and 37. What reason does this phrase give for all that happened?

    b. Look at verse 35. What does John say about his testimony and why does he share it?

John has said before in his Gospel that Jesus was the fulfillment of Scripture, but in this brief passage written during the intensity of the events on the cross, John makes this statement four times in the span of thirteen verses. John knows that while he may have been confused (maybe even hysterical) as the events unfolded, looking back on what he witnessed with his own eyes, he sees that everything unfolded as God intended it to.

2. Turn to Genesis 22:1-14.
    a. In verse 2, God uses two phrases to describe Isaac to Abraham. What two phrases does He use?

    b. Where is Abraham to take his son Isaac, according to this same verse?

    c. For what purpose is Abraham to take Isaac?

3. According to verse 3, how does Abraham respond, and in what time frame?

4. Who and what does Abraham take with him?

5. In verse 5, what does Abraham say he and Isaac are going to do?

6. In verse 6, what does Abraham do with the wood for the burnt offering?

7. What does Isaac ask his father in verse 7?

8. How does Abraham respond in verse 8?

9. According to verse 12, how does God know that Abraham fears Him?

10. Fill in the blanks: And Abraham lifted up his eyes and looked, and behold, behind him was a ram, caught in a thicket by his horns. And Abraham went and took the ram and offered it up as a burnt offering _____ of his _____. (verse 13)

11. What does Abraham call the place and why? (verse 14)

Those who study the Scriptures have a principle of interpretation they refer to as the law of first mention. Basically, it refers to the fact that the simple comes before the complex. There are so many places we see this principle on display. The seed becomes the sprout which grows into a tree with branches, leaves, flowers, and fruit. We see children learn to read by first learning letters and sounds. They combine letters and sounds into words before words are strung together into sentences and paragraphs before becoming complete bodies of works. A study in the development of aviation does not begin with a jumbo jet crossing the Atlantic. Its beginnings are much simpler than that.

Applying the law of first mention to Scripture involves finding the first time a word, concept, or name is mentioned, and studying that passage because it's where you will find the simplest and clearest presentation of a concept that will be more fully developed later on.

12. There are four words or concepts introduced for the first time in this passage of Genesis. With where we are in our study of John at the back of your mind, write down the verse number where these word(s) are first used.
    a. Only son

    b. Whom you love

    c. Burnt offering

    d. worship

God tells Abraham to take his son, his only son. If you're familiar with Abraham's story, you'll know that Abraham has another son; Isaac is not his only son. The wording of this phrase suggests not quantity, but rather quality. Only Isaac is Abraham's one-of-a-kind son of the promise.

And the Word became flesh and dwelt among us, and we have seen his glory, glory as of the only Son from the Father, full of grace and truth. John 1:14

It is also in Genesis 22:2, that we see the word 'love' used for the first time in the Bible.

For God so loved the world, that he gave his only Son, that whoever believes in him should not perish but have eternal life. John 3:16

Before Genesis 22:2, you'll have read about Cain and Abel, and Noah bringing burnt offerings to God. But this is the first time God asked for a sacrifice. And what is perhaps most astonishing of all is that when Abraham left his servants to offer up his son as the sacrifice, he called it an act of worship.

Worship: to honor with extravagant love and extreme submission; as a lover
(Webster's Dictionary, 1828)

And the Scripture, foreseeing that God would justify the Gentiles by faith, preached the gospel beforehand to Abraham, saying, "In you shall all the nations be blessed."
Galatians 3:8

God asked Abraham to sacrifice his one-of-a-kind son, whom he loved, the son of the promise, born to a woman, who in physical terms, was unable to bear a child. Abraham, the man who would be called the father of God's chosen people, responded in obedience. More than that, he considered it an act of worship—an act of extravagant love and extreme devotion—to his God. How Abraham's heart must have ached as he placed the wood for the sacrifice on Isaac's shoulders! How he must have wept as he bound his son to the altar!

But God interrupted this act of obedience and commanded Abraham to stop. God pointed Abraham to a ram and instructed him to sacrifice the ram in place of his son. Can you imagine the joy Abraham must have felt as he freed his son from the altar of sacrifice?! Abraham sacrificed the ram in an act of worship, then called the mountain "the place where the LORD would be seen; the place where God would provide."

About a thousand years later, we encounter another son of promise: Solomon, the promised son of King David. The one God called to build His temple. Do you know where this temple—the building God chose for His glory to dwell—was to be built? On the mountain where the LORD would be seen. (2 Chronicles 3:1)

Fast forward about another thousand years to the day when the true Son of the promise entered the temple. Do you know what He said to religious leaders who knew their Scriptures cold? He said, "Your father Abraham rejoiced that he would see my day. He saw it and was glad." (John 8:56) Jesus tells the descendants of Abraham, that while on the mountain where God would be seen, their father saw the true Lamb. Jesus tells them that Abraham saw a picture of the good news before the fullness of it came.

When the Gospel was preached to Abraham in advance, he saw that in the most extravagant act of love and the most extreme display of devotion, this One-of-a-kind Son of the promise, would carry His cross up another hill, but this time there would be no ram offered in His place. This Son was the Lamb that God promised He would provide. He was the sacrifice who would show God to the world. The knife that did not fall on Isaac would pierce Jesus instead.

Behold your King – God's Lamb – Who takes away the sin of the world

He is Jesus Christ, the one who is truly righteous. He himself is the sacrifice that atones for our sins—and not only our sins but the sins of all the world. 1 John 2:1b, 2 NLT

John had been caught up in confusion and fear when it happened, but looking back, he could see the One to whom all the signs pointed. He had been a witness to the painful journey, but he was also a witness to the beautiful miracle—the birth of the new covenant of grace. John saw and finally understood. What might have seemed slow, confusing, and even painful, had happened at just the right time.

To him who loves us and has freed us from our sins by his blood and made us a kingdom, priests to his God and Father, to him be glory and dominion forever and ever. Amen. Behold, he is coming with the clouds, and every eye will see him . . .Revelation 1:5-7

In the same way, what is yet to come will come at the right time. At times, we may be tempted to confusion and maybe even a little hysteria as we wait. But when the last thread is woven and we see the work completed, it will be breathtakingly beautiful. And it will have been worth the wait.

Day Two: Crucified (John 19:17-42)

In our homework yesterday, we caught a glimpse of how God has worked out the story of redemption from the beginning. We looked at one of the pictures He gave us along the way—a picture of grace, salvation, and love in the story of Abraham and Isaac. Today we turn the lens onto the people who were active participants in, and witnesses to, Christ's death on the cross. You see, every person who was involved had the opportunity to respond to this ultimate display of grace, salvation, and love. They saw the signs. They saw wonders and miracles that could only be explained by divine power, and they made a decision to believe or to disregard what they saw. Either way, a choice was made.

1. Read John 19:17-22.
   a. Who was responsible for the inscription fastened to Jesus' cross?

   b. What did the inscription say?

   c. Who could read the inscription and why were they able to?

   d. How did the chief priests respond?

   e. What did Pilate do about it?

Pilate despised and scorned the Jews. Knowing that he had the power to kill Jesus, but they didn't, he took every opportunity to rub it in their faces. *This is your king. This pathetic man that I have the power to fasten to a cross.* Pilate made sure the Jews knew that they were a powerless people with a powerless king. And Pilate wanted everyone who walked by the spectacle to see and know it too. So Pilate ordered that the inscription hanging above Jesus on the cross be written in Aramaic, the language most commonly understood by Jews, Latin, the official language of Rome, and in Greek, the international language of the empire most widely understood by its citizens.

Though Pilate claimed three times that he found no basis for a charge against Jesus and didn't want Him killed, he still mocked Jesus and the crowd. Pilate was concerned for his own power and position, and when he felt like they were in jeopardy, he handed Jesus over to be crucified. Pilate might have felt like the Jews forced him into killing an innocent man, but he had a choice.

The chief priests might have felt goaded by Pilate into declaring they had no king but Caesar. Maybe they resented Pilate because his power exposed their own greed for it. They might have felt that when Pilate gave them the appearance of power of Jesus' fate, he was forcing their hand. But these men of the book, teachers of the book, enforcers of the book — they had a choice.

2. Read John 19:23-24.
   a. Which group of people is represented in these verses, and what were they doing?

   b. Do you believe they also faced the opportunity to respond personally to what they were witnessing? Use Luke 23:47, Mark 15:39 and Matthew 27:54 to help you with your answer.

They divide my garments among them, and for my clothing they cast lots. Psalm 22:18

The soldiers were part of a story far bigger than they were. But the very fact that they were part of it required their response. They could continue with what seemed the easiest and most expedient action, or they could respond to the awe. Because the thing is, they couldn't miss the awe. They could ignore it and who it pointed to, but they couldn't miss it. Do you know how I know this? If you look back a couple of verses from the one you read in Matthew in the last question, this is what you will read: "And behold, the curtain of the temple was torn in two, from top to bottom. And the earth shook, and the rocks were split. The tombs also were opened. And many bodies of the saints who had fallen asleep were raised, and coming out of the tombs after his resurrection they went into the holy city and appeared to many." (Matthew 27:51-53)

On a Friday afternoon, the world went dark. An earthquake shook the ground. Rocks split and tombs were opened. And many saints who had died now walked around Jerusalem. It seems the only response would be to either close your eyes and plug your ears and pretend it never happened, or to exclaim with at least one of those soldiers, "Surely, this was the Son of God!"

3. Read John 19:25-27. What other group was near the cross as witnesses?

We are going to hear more from some of these people tomorrow, but before we move on, I think it's important to note that these women and the beloved disciple would have been close to Jesus' suffering. We often see paintings depicting Jesus hanging high above the witnesses. In truth, Jesus was probably only about a foot and a half to two feet off of the ground. Those who remained at the foot of the cross were not distant from His suffering.

When I consider the agony of Jesus witnessed by women who loved Him, cared for Him, and likely made the very garments for which the soldiers cast lots, it tears my heart. It would be easier to imagine the scene with distance. It would be easier, but it would not be accurate. Jesus suffered intense anguish for hours, and John and the women remained. Maybe coming and going. Perhaps taking turns supporting the mother who could not leave her Son. But there they stood, witnesses who would not turn away or close their ears to their suffering Saviour. They, too, made a choice.

4. Read John 19:28-30 then look back at John 17:4-5. What do you think is all wrapped up in Jesus' cry, "It is finished"? (There is no way we can answer this completely, but make an attempt.)

Christ our Passover lamb, has been sacrificed. 1 Corinthians 5:7

5. Read John 19:31-37. What did the Jews (meaning Jewish authorities) ask Pilate to do and why did they want him to do it, according to verse 31?

Jewish authorities didn't want their Passover Sabbath to be defiled by criminals on crosses. They asked Pilate to break their legs to speed up death. But Jesus had already given up His spirit. The Promised Son, the Lamb sacrificed in place of sinful humanity, had already died. The Jews would go home to commemorate the time God delivered them from slavery in peace because Jesus was finally dead. They would gather with their families over a lamb with no physical defects or blemishes, a lamb that could have none of its bones broken, as the true Passover Lamb, beaten and torn without one of His bones being broken, died to free them from slavery to sin and death.

(The Passover Lamb) shall be eaten in one house; you shall not take any of the flesh outside the house, and you shall not break any of its bones. Exodus 12:46

He keeps all his bones; not one of them is broken. Psalm 34:20

6. Read John 19:38-42.
   a. What do you know about Joseph of Arimathea from these verses?

   b. What else do you learn about him from Luke 23:50-51?

c. What do you know about Nicodemus from these verses?

d. What else do you learn about him from John 3:1?

Your throne, O God, is forever and ever. The scepter of your kingdom is a scepter of uprightness; you have loved righteousness and hated wickedness. Therefore God, your God, has anointed you with the oil of gladness beyond your companions; your robes are all fragrant with myrrh and aloes and cassia. Psalm 45:6-8

Both Joseph and Nicodemus had, for a time, stayed distant from the controversy surrounding who Jesus was. But on this beautiful, terrible day, they could no longer sit back and observe complacently. The time had come for them to enter the story with a personal response. A response that would come at great cost to them. There was costliness in the sheer amount of spices. There was a cost in going to Pilate for permission to care for Jesus' body. They were now connected to Jesus in a way that would not have escaped the notice of their fellow Jewish rulers. On that night, Joseph and Nicodemus both knew they had encountered the Son of God and there was no such thing as a neutral response.

As has happened throughout our study in John's Gospel, the spotlight now shines on us.

7. What about you? Have you honestly examined the evidence? If you have, and decide against it, you are free to make that choice. But if you have come to see truth in Jesus' claims, what impact will that have on how you live?

There will come a day when our response will be required. You may be able to put off a decision for a time, but when He returns in all His glory, there will be no mistaking that He is who He said He was: the Son of God.

Therefore God has highly exalted him and bestowed on him the name that is above every name, so that at the name of Jesus every knee should bow, in heaven and on earth and under the earth, and every tongue confess that Jesus Christ is Lord, to the glory of God the Father. Philippians 2:9-11

Day Three: Woman, Why Are You Weeping? (John 20:1-18)

Now on the first day of the week Mary Magdalene came to the tomb early, while it was still dark . . . (John 20:1)

Let's start today by doing a short character sketch of this Mary who was at the tomb early.

1. Look up Luke 8:2-3, Matthew 27:55-56, 61, and John 19:25. What do we learn about Mary Magdalene from these references?

Mary had been bound up by the forces of evil. She had known darkness and slavery and oppression. Then, one day, her Rescuer came and set her free. It seems that from the moment Jesus freed her, she bound herself to Him.

2. Read John 20:1-10.
   a. When does Mary go to Jesus' tomb, and what does she find? (verse 1)

   b. What does Mary do in response to this discovery? (verse 2)

   c. What does Mary say to Simon Peter and John in verse 2?

   d. Look more closely at Mary's words: what does she think has happened to the body?

   e. What do Peter and John find after investigating the situation?

---

f. Mary saw the empty tomb and thought someone had taken the body. What was John's response, according to verse 8? Explain.

g. What do the disciples still not understand at this point, according to verse 9?

Mary, Peter, and John were all eyewitnesses to the horror of Jesus' crucifixion on Friday. The One they had followed was dead. When Joseph of Arimathea and Nicodemus took Jesus' body from the cross, prepared it, and laid it in the tomb, Mary was there. She had seen Jesus' body wrapped in linen and spices. But her plan was to go back. To do more? To do better? Maybe she didn't feel like the men had done a good enough job with Jesus. Maybe she felt the job had been rushed. Maybe she just felt like she, herself, needed to care for the man who'd cared for her.

Whatever the reason, Mary waited through the Sabbath as the Scriptures told her to. (Luke 23:56) Did she "celebrate" the Passover together with her family? Did she gather together over a lamb, as God's lamb lay broken for her?

On the first day of the week, before the sun was even up but after the Son had already risen, Mary returned to the last place she'd been with Jesus.

She went back to Jesus' tomb, but found nothing as she expected it would be. Jesus was not where they had left Him. John 19:41 tells us that Jesus' body had been the only one in that tomb. It was common for several bodies to be placed in the same tomb and if Jesus' body had been one among others, it would have been a lot harder to determine He wasn't there anymore. Mary knew this is not what had happened.

Peter and John looked into the tomb Mary said was empty. They saw the linen clothes lying there, but the body was gone. They knew this wasn't a grave robbing. They'd seen first-hand the power of the men responsible for Jesus' death. These men had gone to great lengths to make sure the body of the man who'd publicly and repeatedly said He would die, but wouldn't stay dead, wouldn't cause them even more trouble by disappearing. (Matthew 27:62-66)

No, this was no grave robbing. John saw the empty tomb and believed. He didn't fully understand how this fulfilled Scripture or what it meant for them specifically and the world generally, but he believed that Jesus was no longer dead.

3. Read John 20:11-15.
   a. What are the first two words of John 20:11? (ESV)

   b. Mary stays behind when Peter and John leave. What does she see when she looks in the tomb?

c. What question do the angels ask Mary, and how does she respond?

d. What happens immediately after her encounter with the angels? (verse 14)

e. What two questions does Jesus ask Mary, and how does she answer Him?

4. Look at John 1:38. What question does Jesus first ask the disciples? How does Jesus rephrase this question in John 18:4, 7 and John 20:15?

Mary is single-minded in her devotion and she will not leave until she finds Jesus. She knows that the answer to what she is looking for is actually a who—it's Jesus.

5. Read John 20:16-18.
   a. What one word does Jesus say that causes Mary to recognize Him for who He is?

   b. Flip back to John 10:2-4. How does this passage develop John 20:16 more fully?

   c. Why do you think Jesus says what He does to Mary in verse 17? (This is a very tough question so, again, don't focus on trying to figure out the "right" answer. Think about it in terms of all we've studied so far and try to put your learning together.)

The One who knew her heart and therefore knew what she sought, came to her and called her by name. Jesus, the Chief Shepherd, had laid down His life for His sheep, and when He called this one sad and crying sheep by name, she immediately knew who He was.

6. Fill in the blank with your own name: Jesus said to her, "_____."

Just as Jesus called Mary by name, He calls each of us—intimately and individually.

Some day, all who understand that what they are seeking is actually a who—Jesus—will also hear Him speak their name. I can't help but look forward to the day I lay down to sleep, only to be stirred awake by the sound of my name, spoken by a voice I have never heard, but one I will know in an instant.

On that day, I, who have the privilege of knowing, reading, and believing the Scriptures, will be able to cling to Him.

Mary tried to hold onto Him, but she was still trying to hold on to what had been. She thought Jesus was back and everything could finally return to normal, to how things had been before the cross. But there was no going back to what was. And that isn't a sad thing! What was coming, and had now come, was better! Mary clearly had a big view of Jesus, as evidenced by her commitment and devotion. But her picture of Him still wasn't big enough.

What Mary was an eyewitness to was not just, as Carson says, her "private dream-come-true." It was the good news that needed to be shared because it was for everyone.

7.   What does Mary do in verse 18, once she has seen the One she is looking for?

We have come full circle from where we started. All are invited to come and see. Those who see the One that Scripture proclaims and to whom the signs point, are instructed to go and tell.

**How beautiful on the mountains are the feet of those who bring good news, who proclaim peace, who bring good tidings, who proclaim salvation, who say to Zion, "Your God reigns!"
Isaiah 52:7**

My deepest prayer is that we will not have spent this time studying the Scriptures only to walk away with information we didn't have before. My prayer is that we will be able to say with Mary, "I have seen the Lord!" We won't understand fully and completely on our first glance. We won't understand it while we're still breathing. But our Helper will not leave us until the day we hear Jesus call our name, and we see Him face to face. The Holy Spirit will guide us deeper into the truth of Jesus until that day. A truth too amazing to not share with everyone. So come and see, and then go and tell!

That which we have seen and heard we proclaim also to you, so that you too may have fellowship with us; and indeed our fellowship is with the Father and with his Son Jesus Christ. 1 John 1:3

Day Four: My Lord and My God! (John 20:19-29)

The passage we are studying today picks up on Resurrection Sunday, the evening of the same day Mary Magdalene found the empty tomb. The same day Jesus stood before her and called her by name. The same day she declared, most likely with joy and trembling, "I have seen the Lord!"

1. Read John 20:19-23.
   a. What does verse 19 tell us about the place the disciples were gathered?

   b. What reason is given for this safety measure?

   c. Knowing the doors were locked, what can you infer about how Jesus enters the home?

   d. What does Jesus say to the disciples at the end of verse 19, in response to their fear?

2. Flip back to John 14:27 and John 16:33. Both of these verses come from the context of Jesus teaching His disciples and preparing them for what will happen at the cross. By telling them ahead of time, He is encouraging them not to lose heart. How do you think Jesus' words to His disciples at the end of John 20:19 took on new meaning when they heard Him speak to them on this side of the cross?

Though at least two of the disciples had seen the empty tomb with their own eyes, though they had the eyewitness testimony of Mary Magdalene, who announced that she had not just seen the empty tomb, but she had also seen Jesus (verse 18), the disciples were still gathered behind locked doors in fear.

They'd seen firsthand a reason for fear. With their own eyes they'd seen the tribulation of the world. But they had not yet experienced a definitive reason to take heart. They still were not sure that Jesus had overcome the world. Maybe Mary was right and He was alive. He certainly wasn't in the tomb. But had He really overcome the world?

3. What does Jesus do immediately after saying, "Peace be with you"?

4. How does verse 20 describe the disciples' emotions after seeing their Lord?

So also you have sorrow now, but I will see you again, and your hearts will rejoice, and no one will take your joy from you! John 16:22

Jesus knew what was in the hearts and minds of His disciples without them having to tell Him. He addressed their questions, doubts, and fears with solid proof. Irrefutable evidence. John 19:32-34 tells us that the men who died with Jesus had their legs broken, but they did not have their sides pierced. Jesus, however, was pierced for our transgressions, yet not one of His bones was broken. And we read in John 19:35 that at least one of the men in the room that night had seen the crucifixion with his own eyes. Jesus is giving them hard, solid evidence that He is the one who was on that cross.

5. What instruction does Jesus give His disciples at the end of verse 21?

6. What does Jesus do in verse 22 in response to the commission He has just laid out for the disciples?

7. What words does Jesus follow this act with?

8. Turn to Genesis 2:7. What happens in this verse, and how do you think it connects with what Jesus does in Question #6?

In the beginning was the Word, and the Word was with God, and the Word was God. He was in the beginning with God. All things were made through him, and without him was not any thing made that was made. In him was life, and the life was the light of men. The light shines in the darkness, and the darkness has not overcome it. John 1:1-5

The Light of the World stood among them as proof that darkness had been overcome. Death was defeated. Light and Life would have the final word because the Word was God.

When the resurrected Christ stood among them, He pierced the darkness of fear with Light. When the Man they'd seen crucified breathed on them, He blew away the power of death with the breath of Life. Jesus gave those disciples peace that overcame fear and resulted in joy. Peace no one could take away. Now they were to live in this peace and spread it.

As you sent me into the world, so I have sent them into the world. John 17:18

Jesus' mission was not over, even though His time on earth soon would be. His mission would continue through His disciples, through men and women who'd seen with their own eyes, and who were carried by the wind of the Spirit.

But when the Helper comes, whom I will send to you from the Father, the Spirit of truth, who proceeds from the Father, he will bear witness about me. And you also will bear witness, because you have been with me from the beginning. John 15:26-27

When those disciples felt the breath of Jesus upon them, I wonder if they immediately pictured the valley of dry bones from Ezekiel 37? Ezekiel had been given words about a time when the people would be sprinkled with water and made clean. A time when they'd have new hearts of flesh. A time when God would put His Spirit within them and they'd walk in God's ways.

But Ezekiel lived among stubborn and rebellious people and this must have seemed almost impossible. Until God came to him in a vision and brought Ezekiel to a valley filled with very dry bones. God asked Ezekiel if he thought the bones could live. Ezekiel answered, "O Lord GOD, you know." (I wonder if this was Ezekiel's way of saying that he had no idea what the right answer was in this situation?)

God told Ezekiel to prophesy over the bones and say to them, "O dry bones, hear the word of the LORD. Thus says the Lord GOD to these bones: 'Behold, I will cause breath to enter you, and you shall live, and you shall know that I am the LORD.'" (Ezekiel 37:4-6)

Ezekiel obeyed and, before his eyes, the bones came together. Sinews came upon them, then flesh, then skin. The valley of dry bones was now a valley of corpses. But they were still dead. This is what we read next:

Then he said to me, "Prophesy to the breath; prophesy, son of man, and say to the breath, Thus says the LORD GOD: Come from the four winds, O breath, and breathe on these slain, that they may live." So I prophesied as he commanded me, and the breath came into them, and they lived and stood on their feet, an exceedingly great army. Ezekiel 37:9-10b

I can't help but wonder if, after Jesus died, the disciples felt a little like that valley of dry bones and corpses. Dead. Lost hope. Bleak future. And then Jesus stood with them — the One who was

181

crucified and could show them the scars to prove it. The One who is the Breath of Life—through whom all things have their being—breathed on them! I wonder if, in that moment, they caught a glimpse of an exceedingly great army?!

9. Read John 20:24-31.

   a. Who enters the scene here, and what do the disciples tell him?

   b. How does he respond?

   c. How long does he live with his response?

   d. Jesus appears to them again. What does He ask Thomas to do?

   e. What does Jesus say to Thomas at the end of verse 27?

Thomas often gets a bad rap, you know, with the whole Doubting Thomas thing. But maybe we should cut him some slack. The other disciples didn't believe Mary's testimony when she shared it with them. They, too, had to see with their own eyes first. So even though Thomas would have had the benefit of more eyewitness testimony than they did, he hadn't seen with his own eyes like they had.

Here's the thing, and it's important: as we conclude our study in the Gospel of John, we need to know that when God calls people to believe in Him by putting their faith in His Son, Jesus, He never calls anyone to blind faith. He never encourages anyone to take wild and crazy leaps or to rely on quickly-changing or mystical feelings. Never. Not once.

From beginning to end, God shows who He is and explains who He is before He calls people to follow Him. The patriarchs heard God, saw His works, were told what would come, then watched it come true. God showed His people incredible signs before asking them to walk out of slavery in Egypt and follow Him into the freedom of the Promised Land. Leaders, judges, kings, prophets, and ordinary men and women were all given revelation and information before they were asked to respond.

Eight weeks ago you responded to the invitation to come and see. The trial is over and a verdict must be declared. How will you respond? Will you respond like Thomas, "My Lord and my God!"? Will you believe that Jesus is the Christ, the One the prophets and Scriptures foretold? Will you believe that life is only found in Him? Will you see that He has come from the Father to make Him known? You have eyewitness testimony—what will you do with it?

We've come to the end of our study and it's time to put down this book.

Pick up the Bible. Open its pages and examine the evidence because our response has eternal consequences. Start again with man's first breath in the garden and read until the day the hand of God wipes the last tear away. Encounter the Christ and let Him shine His light on you.

Then turn and shine it on your world. You have come and seen, now go and tell. Don't worry about your telling looking "big" as the world defines it. Abide. Grow. Breathe in His grace and breathe out His praise. Spread the breath of life to those around you.

And we know that the Son of God has come and has given us understanding, so that we may know him who is true; and we are in him who is true, in his Son Jesus Christ. He is the true God and eternal life. 1 John 5:20

And this is eternal life, that they know you, the only true God, and Jesus Christ whom you have sent. John 17:3

Day Five: Personal Reflection

For all the promises of God find their Yes in him. That is why it is through him that we utter our Amen to God for his glory. 2 Corinthians 1:20

This final week of our study in John has been a commotion of extremes. The disciples experienced both height and depth of emotion as they watched what looked like pandemonium. At first, their Messiah seemed to fall spectacularly short of all their expectations. But then, after the most significant sign, Jesus Christ revealed Himself to be the conqueror of death and the risen Lord in a plan known to God since the very beginning! Those who'd looked to God throughout all the Scriptures, who'd waited for the fulfillment of the promises, now heard, "It is finished!" All promises find their YES in Christ, even those still awaiting fulfillment. God is glorified in Him, so we can say, "Amen!"

Our prayer for you, as you've diligently sought to discover who Jesus is, echoes the words of Paul:

I have not stopped thanking God for you, I pray for you constantly, asking God, the glorious Father of our Lord Jesus Christ, to give you spiritual wisdom and insight so that you might grow in your knowledge of God. I pray that your hearts will be flooded with light so that you can understand the confident hope he has given to those he called — his holy people who are his rich and glorious inheritance. I also pray that you will understand the incredible greatness of God's power for us who believe him. This is the same mighty power that raised Christ from the dead and seated him in the place of honor at God's right hand in the heavenly realms. Ephesians 1:16-20 NLT

We have come, and we have seen. It's time to respond. We've seen how those in Scripture responded to the revealed Jesus in both the New and Old Testaments. Now it is your turn.

1. Jesus posed the question: "What are you seeking?" The NIV words it, "What is it you want?" This question is for you as well. Spend some time in prayer as you consider your answer. Are you coming to Jesus because you want more of Him? More of His presence? Is it Him you seek, or just what He can do for you? What's the practical difference between wanting Him versus wanting something *from* Him?

2. He has shown you who He is. How will you respond? Will you worship, declaring, "My Lord and my God!"? What will you give up — disbelief, doubt? As the Father sent the Son, how does He want to send you out? How will you go and tell so that others might believe and have life in His name?

... Blessed are those who have not seen and yet have believed. John 20:29

Teaching Session Nine: Follow Me! (John 21)

- ❖ Jesus knew the time had come for Him to leave and for the Holy Spirit to take over.

- ❖ Peter had publicly declared that he was willing to die for Jesus. He had said that even if all of the other disciples abandoned Jesus, he never would. But he had also denied Jesus just as publicly. Not once, or twice, but three times. As the leader of this group of disciples, Peter needed to be restored publicly if he was going to be able to finish what had been started.

- ❖ Three times Jesus asks Peter if he loves Him. Three times Peter answers yes, you know I do. For Peter to finish what had been started, he would need to be firmly rooted in his love for Jesus.

- ❖ Jesus reinstates Peter by assuring that Peter is grounded in love for Him, that he understands his role as an under-shepherd caring for the sheep of the Chief Shepherd, and that he, Peter, would actually lay down his life for Christ when the time came.

"When you are old, you will stretch out your hands, and another will dress you and carry you where you do not want to go"… And after saying this he said to him, "Follow me." John 21:18

- ❖ If Peter is going to obey Jesus' command to follow, it will mean following even to the cross.

- ❖ How does this change Peter? He becomes a message of encouragement and hope to those suffering under persecution.

Therefore, let those who suffer according to God's will entrust their souls to a faithful Creator while doing good. Acts 4:19

And after you have suffered a little while, the God of all grace, who has called you to his eternal glory in Christ, will himself restore, confirm, strengthen, and establish you. To him be the dominion forever and ever. Amen. 1 Peter 5:10-11

- ❖ Empowered by the Holy Spirit, Peter became the rock Jesus had said he would be. He loved Jesus, cared for His sheep, and followed Him, even to the cross. Peter finished what he'd been called to do.

- ❖ Peter was to be a leader and a martyr and John was going to live a long life of enduring witness.

This is the disciple who is bearing witness about these things, and who has written these things, and we know that his testimony is true. John 21:24

❖ John had done what he'd been sent to do. He'd written what he'd witnessed. And he ends with Jesus—the Word, through whom all things were created, but the One who can't be contained by words.

That which was from the beginning, which we have heard, which we have seen with our eyes, which we looked upon and have touched without hands…we proclaim also to you, so that you too may have fellowship with us. 1 John 1:1, 3

❖ **What are you projects?**
  ◆ Look at them through God's eyes. Can you see they're not yours but His? And if they're His projects then it's up to Him to bring them to completion in His way. He will. You can trust that.

❖ **John's Message:**
  ◆ When we see who He is, when we believe He is who He says He is, and then we see what He's done, we'll fall in love with the One who loved us first and we'll be changed. Anything we are called to do for Him after that will be a response of love.

Anyone who loves me will obey my teaching. John 14:23 NIV

❖ Jesus told His disciples on the night before the cross that if they loved Him they'd obey Him. What they knew about Him in their minds would grow affection for Him in their hearts, and would cause them to act in such a way that people would see who they belonged to.

❖ Rules don't change people, love does.

❖ If our projects are His projects, we will have to trust what He is doing and how and when He is doing it. Our job is to spend our days coming to Him to see Him. Our job is to grow in relationship with Him and let His love change us and change our story. That's how coming and seeing leads to going and telling.

We live out the greatest love story of all: we love Him because He loved us first.

View this teaching session at www.unshakenministries.com

Session Notes:

_____

_____

_____

_____

_____

_____

_____

_____

_____

_____

_____

_____

_____

_____

_____

_____

_____

_____

_____

_____

_____

_____

_____

_____

What then shall we say to these things? If God is for us,
who can be against us?
He who did not spare His own Son but gave Him up for us all,
how will He not also with Him graciously give us all things?

Who shall bring any charge against God's elect?
It is God who justifies.

Who is to condemn?
Christ Jesus is the One who died—more than that, who was raised—who is at the right hand of
God, who indeed is interceding for us.

Who shall separate us from the love of Christ?
No, in all these things were are more than conquerors through Him who loved us.
For I am sure that neither death nor life, nor angels nor rulers, nor things present nor things to
come, nor powers, nor height nor depth, nor anything else in all creation, will be able to
separate us from the love of God in Christ Jesus our Lord.
Romans 8:31-39

References

Carson, D. (1991). *The Gospel According to John.* Grand Rapids, Michigan: William B. Eerdmans Publishing Company.

Carson, D. (2001, 01 1). *The Gospel Coalition.* Retrieved from Part 5: Jesus the Bread of God (john 6:25-71 Series: Portraits of Jesus in John's Gospel: www.resources.thegospelcoalition.org

Erica Friedman, T. L. (2014, November 21). *Is there such a thing as a stupid or dumb question?* Retrieved June 26, 2017, from Quora: www.quora.com

Kostenbergen, A. J. (2004). *John.* Grand Rapids, Michigan: Baker Academic.

Reiner, R. (Director). (1992). *A Few Good Men* [Motion Picture].

Shyamalan, M. N. (Director). (1999). *The Sixth Sense* [Motion Picture].

Manufactured by Amazon.ca
Acheson, AB